SHRUBS

FOR BLOOM AND BEAUTY

HIBISCUS rosa-sinensis 'Fiesta'

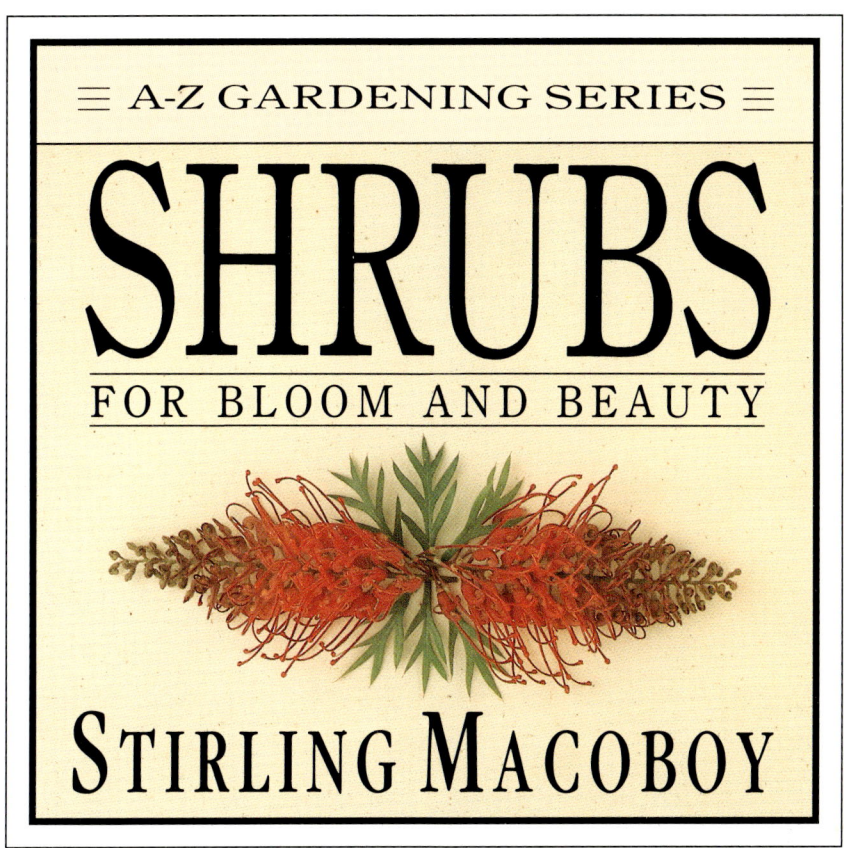

≡ A-Z GARDENING SERIES ≡

SHRUBS

FOR BLOOM AND BEAUTY

STIRLING MACOBOY

ANGUS
& ROBERTSON
PUBLISHERS

ANGUS & ROBERTSON PUBLISHERS

Unit 4, Eden Park, 31 Waterloo Road,
North Ryde, NSW, Australia 2113;
94 Newton Road, Auckland 1,
New Zealand; and
16 Golden Square, London W1R 4BN,
United Kingdom

First published by Lansdowne Press, Sydney, in 1984
First published in Australia
by Angus & Robertson Publishers in 1989
First published in New Zealand
by Angus & Robertson NZ Ltd in 1989

Copyright © Stirling Macoboy 1984

National Library of Australia
Cataloguing-in-publication data.

Macoboy, Stirling, 1927-
 Shrubs for bloom and beauty.

 Includes index.
 ISBN 0 207 15901 7.

 1. Flowering shrubs. 2. Ornamental shrubs. I. Macoboy,
 Stirling, 1927-   . Flowering shrubs. II. Title. III.
 Title: Flowering shrubs. (Series: Macoboy, Stirling,
 1927-   . A-Z gardening series).

635.9'76

Line drawings by Murray Frederick

Printed in Singapore

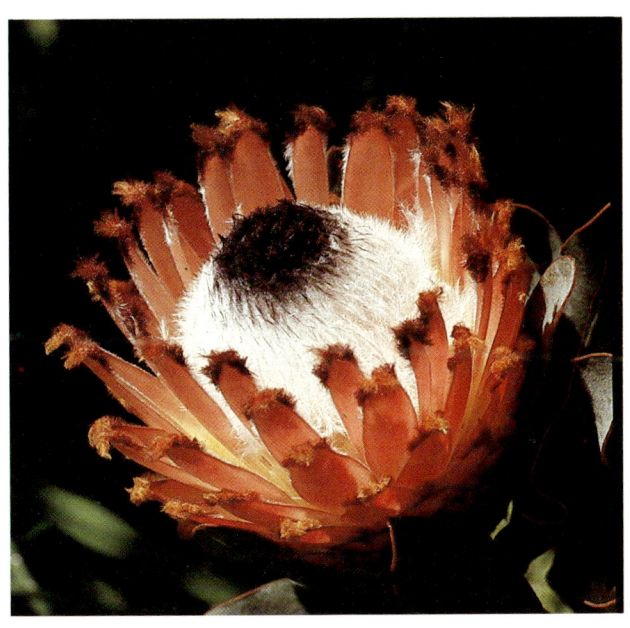

CONTENTS

ACKNOWLEDGEMENTS

Not all plants shown in this book will be available in every country in which the book is sold. Some may even be restricted. Lovely *Lavandula stoechas* for instance, and the Scottish Broom, *Cytisus scoparius,* are classed as noxious weeds in some parts of Australia. The photographs were taken in many different gardens in many different countries. Among the major locations were:

In the United States
At the Brooklyn Botanic Garden, New York; at the Descanso Gardens, the Huntington Gardens, La Brea Park, Los Angeles State and Country Arboretum, the Pacific Coast Botanic Gardens, the Rancho Santa Ana, the Santa Barbara Botanic Garden, the UCLA Botanic Garden, all in southern California; the Strybing Arboretum, San Francisco.

In France
At the Jardin Botanique, Paris; L'Hay les Roses, and at Malmaison and Bagatelle.

In Australia
At the Brisbane Botanic Gardens, the Oasis and the St Bernard Hotel, Mt Tamborine, in Queensland. The National Botanic Garden, A.C.T. The Royal Botanic Gardens and Hyde Park, Sydney; Eryldene, Gordon; Milton Park and Retford Park, Bowral; Lindfield Park, Mt Wilson; Stony Range Reserve, Dee Why; the Four Seasons Nursery, Sorensons' Blue Mountains Nursery, all in N.S.W.

In England
At the Beth Chatto Garden, Essex; the Chelsea Flower Show; Hidcote, Gloucestershire; the RHS Garden, Wisley, Surrey; Queen Mary's Rose Garden, Regent's Park; the Royal Botanic Garden, Kew; Spalding, Lincs; the Harry Wheatcroft Nursery, Notts.

In Ireland
At Ilnacullin, Garinish, Co. Cork; the Irish National Botanic Garden, Glasnevin; Powerscourt, Co. Wicklow; St Stephen's Green and Merrion Square, Dublin.

In Asia
At the Hong Kong Botanic Garden, and the Kadoorie Farm and Botanic Gardens; at the Shinjuku Go-en and Tokyo Botanic Garden; the Singapore Botanic Gardens; the University of the Philippines, Makiling.

In the Pacific
At the Jardin Botanique de Tahiti; Honolulu's Foster Gardens and the Wahiawa Botanic Garden, Hawaii.

Other species were photographed in my own garden and at those of friends, both old and new. My thanks to the volunteer chauffeurs without whose efforts many of the pictures might have remained untaken.

Contents Page: *PROTEA barbigera*

INTRODUCTION

WHAT IS A SHRUB?

A garden without shrubs? Impossible to visualize! If trees form the bones or skeleton of garden design, then shrubs must surely be considered the flesh in any climatic zone. In nature, they form the mid-story—lower than the trees, taller than the small plants that clothe the actual ground surface. See the way they soften the height-gap between trees and grasses at the edge of any forest, the way they frame a pathway, beckoning you onward along a track they have chosen to mark so colourfully. Notice the way they reduce the apparent height of a rocky outcrop by clustering at its base, or the manner in which they seem to flatten out a bank by spilling down its face. You'll find them reflecting in pools, clustering along coastal rocks, lining streambeds, hanging over mountain trails. Anywhere there's a space available between those invaluable, shade-giving green giants, the trees.

Now think a moment—don't the descriptions of idealized shrub-places above suggest corners of any well-planned garden? Softening the lines of your house . . . framing a path or view, mirrored in a pond, sprawling over a bank . . . surely your garden has places just like that, which could benefit from the placement of a colourful, flower-bearing shrub to spill fragrance in your way as you move about.

All those and more!

Shrubs will bring many changes to your garden—not least of them the butterflies that hover above the blooms on summer days, the small birds that find food and shelter among the low branches: you provide the shelter, they'll help keep your yard insect free!

Most of the flowering shrubs you'll find in this book are fast-growing too, generally reaching reasonable (if not maximum) size in just a few years. And with an occasional pruning and a regular ration of plant food they'll flourish throughout your lifetime and beyond it—not like those other plants that need replacing every year or so.

A large proportion of shrubs are easy to propagate too, meaning they can be grown from cuttings or divisions, so that you can literally increase your stock without financial outlay. This ease of propagation is usually reflected in the prices at your local nursery. A small shrub, promising a lifetime of flowers and fragrance, can often be bought for the same price as a similarly-sized herb or houseplant, which may only last a single season.

What then is a shrub? How does one tell it from other types of plants? In truth, there is no clear, scientific distinction. Both trees and shrubs are tough plants whose woody stems often help them survive winter in frost-prone areas, where more succulent plants would be destroyed.

Some shrubs grow as tall as any tree, and vice versa. But a shrub as most of us would visualize it is a woody plant of more delicate habit than a tree, and without an obvious trunk. Sometimes it has many trunks arising from the same set of roots, like an oleander or a rose. At other times it develops a low, branching habit like a gardenia, so that its single trunk is well disguised, even at ground level. Shrubs from cold climates are inclined to be deciduous, often expanding their short flowering span with a respectable crop of fruit or berries, and later, dazzling the eye with autumn colour. Tropical or warm temperate shrubs don't have to worry about frost damage, and produce splendid evergreen foliage that is sometimes colourful in itself. Often their blooming is prolonged throughout the warmer months, even the whole year in a suitable climate.

Small trees can be trained into bushy shrubs by cutting the main trunk back early in life and forcing a branched habit. Contrariwise, many shrubs can be turned into small trees by standardizing them: that is to say, by gradually removing all branches up to a height of say, two metres. A tree from one climate may decide to adopt a shrubby habit elsewhere, perhaps in an exposed position. Any true distinction, then, between trees and shrubs is yet to be discovered. And all existing distinctions might be said to owe more to man than to nature. One thing we can all agree on is their extraordinary beauty.

HOW TO GROW FLOWERING SHRUBS

The major part of any well-organized planting will consist of shrubs. Usually seen at or near eye-level, they provide the largest colour display, and if skilfully chosen can produce a succession of bloom throughout the year. Most shrubs however spend much of the year bare of flowers, so it is wise to choose from those that are also attractive out of bloom. Consider the size, shape, texture and colour of the foliage. Unusually coloured leaves can be just as eye-catching as flowers and are visible for at least eight months of the year. If they change colour with the seasons, so much the better. Many shrubs produce brightly coloured berries or other decorative fruits, which keep the plant attractive long after the flowers have finished and may also lure birds into the garden.

Consider, too, the natural shape of a shrub, especially if you are planting for a specific purpose such as a windbreak, an accent feature, or merely as a background for flowers. If you are planting a lawn specimen, you'll want to be sure that the shrub you choose has a pleasing silhouette; windbreaks will require a fairly dense, compact shape; shrubs to backdrop flower displays should not be too showy when out of bloom, and must have leaves of a colour that complements or contrasts with the flower display.

Choosing shrubs

What you attempt to grow should be largely dictated by the climate in which you live. Shrubs are found in all parts of the world, and while many are adaptable, best results are always achieved in climates similar to that of the plant's natural home. Tropical and subtropical shrubs can rarely survive frost, and deciduous shrubs may not colour well in warm-temperate to hotter areas. Other factors that should influence your choice are your rainfall pattern and soil type. A shrub of tropical origin needs its rain in summer, with dry, warm weather in winter, while a mild temperate climate gives just the opposite: a dry summer, a soaking wet and cold winter.

If you live in a dry area, it could be foolish to plant a rainforest shrub — unless you're prepared to spend hours on daily watering throughout the summer. Likewise, if your soil is poorly drained clay, choose shrubs that occur naturally in similar soil, rather than those which prefer well-drained sand. Alternatively, you could change your soil to suit the shrubs! Boggy soil can be drained with agricultural pipes, and heavy clay lightened by working gypsum, sand and compost into it. An easier way of improving drainage is to build garden beds up to about 30cm above natural soil level. Shrubs can be planted in the new top layer, and excess water will drain away from the roots.

Once you have narrowed down your list to shrubs suitable for your climate and soil, select for size and shape, timing of flowers and fruit. By knowing as much about each shrub's habit as possible, you can choose plants that are right for specific purposes and have a garden that flowers on cue. You may like a garden that bursts into bloom in spring, or prefer a succession of flowers all year. Whatever you want is possible *provided* you get to know your shrubs before planting. You will certainly need to know what size they grow so you can calculate how many to buy and how far apart to plant them.

Shrubs should be planted so their branches intertwine when mature, but not so closely that they crowd each other into a shapeless mass. Plant too closely, and you will have to dig some out later to give the others growing room. Plant too far apart and the mature garden will look unnatural, like a station waiting for the train to come in.

Buying shrubs

When you've decided on the shrubs you want, check each one over carefully before you actually buy. Be sure they look healthy and are well-furnished with leaves and branches. Beware of yellowing leaves and broken wood. Check for signs of insect infestation such as holes in leaves or mottling. Don't buy shrubs grown to a large size in small containers. Such shrubs usually progress poorly when planted out, for their roots have been too compacted.

In Europe and in the United States where winters are very cold, deciduous shrubs are often sold bare-rooted. These shrubs are cheaper, lighter and

 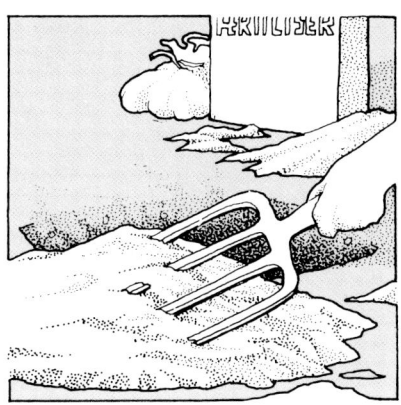 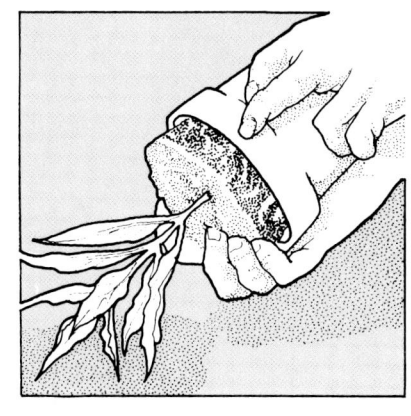

easier to handle, but their roots must still be wrapped to protect them from drying out. Don't buy if the roots have been exposed to sun and air.

Bare-rooted shrubs are available only from late autumn through winter, when they are dormant; they must be planted immediately. Container-grown shrubs are available any time, but obviously the best specimens of any plant are displayed at nurseries when they are in bloom, so they should be bought at that time. Planting them out during the mild seasons, autumn and spring, generally gives the best results.

Planting shrubs

Thorough soil preparation before you plant will ensure that your shrubs get off to the best possible start. Dig the holes twice as wide and deep as the container dimensions or the root mass. Break up any

D: Planting bare-root. Set root mass on mound in hole.

E: Ball and burlapped. Wrapping will rot away after planting.

F: Carefully lower unpotted root mass into hole: check level.

A: Dig a hole twice as wide and deep as the container.

B: Fork over soil, add compost and manure, reserve for planting.

C: Slide shrub out of container (easiest just after watering).

clods and work some well-rotted manure or compost into the soil taken from the hole. Half-fill the hole with this enriched soil and firm down.

Should staking be necessary, drive the stakes into the bottom of the hole before half-refilling with soil and before the shrub is planted. Then there is no risk of piercing or tearing the roots. Ensure that the stake is no closer than 10cm/4in from the trunk, and fix the shrub to it with ties that will not cut into the bark. Old stockings are a perfect choice for this.

If your land is flat and you are digging straight down into heavy clay—stop! Holes dug in clay fill quickly with water after heavy rain and drain only slowly if at all. Most shrubs cannot stand wet feet and soon drown in poorly drained beds. Either set in drainage channels below the deepest roots, or consider building raised garden beds with good quality, porous soil.

Water the shrub in its container and tap sharply several times so that the roots and soil separates

from the pot in one mass. Slide it out gently with as little disturbance as possible.

Place the root mass in the hole, adjusting the soil level so that the trunk of the shrub is no deeper into the soil than it was in the container. Water the roots and soil in the half-filled hole, then refill with the remaining soil, firm down and water again. Tamp the soil into a dish-shaped depression around the trunk so as to hold and direct water to where it is needed most.

Bare-root shrubs need to be planted slightly differently. Build a cone-shaped mound in the half-filled hole and place the shrub on top, spreading the roots down and outward all around. Be sure to force soil in and around all roots so that no air pockets remain, firm down and water well. Refill the hole and water again.

Shrubs sold with their roots wrapped in hessian (balled and burlapped) can be treated as container plants, but there is no need to remove the wrapping—it will quickly rot away when covered.

Benefits of mulching

Shrubs grow better if the surrounding soil is kept cool and moist, free of competing weeds, and fertile. Happily there is an easy way to ensure all these and utilize bulky garden and organic household wastes as well—it is called mulching. Mulch can be any material laid on the soil to inhibit evaporation, reduce fluctuations in soil temperature and suppress weeds. Pebbles and even horticultural polythene are sometimes used, but organic mulches such as compost, rotted manure, bark chips and leaf mould are the best because they also supply plant nutrients and encourage useful soil organisms. Compost can be made at home, without cost, from grass clippings and leafy kitchen waste. Fallen leaves can either be added to these in a compost heap, or raked directly around shrubs.

In summer, mulch keeps the soil cool and moist, and in cold winter areas can prevent the ground from freezing, thus preserving the roots of some shrubs normally too tender for such harsh conditions. Apply mulch in a layer at least 10cm/4in thick, right around the shrub out to the edge of the foliage. Keep it clear of the trunk or you may encourage stem-rotting fungus diseases. With *Azaleas* and other surface-rooting shrubs be careful not to lay the mulch in too deep a layer, as this can encourage the roots to travel upwards, and lead to death of the lower root system. Rake away last year's mulch before adding a new layer.

Watering

Young shrubs should be watered deeply and regularly for at least a year after planting so that they become well established. Deep soakings encourage the formation of good root systems—light sprinklings only

Spectacular spring show of *Azalea indica* along the Epping Highway, Lane Cove, N.S.W.

encourage surface roots which dry out in hot weather. In any case, the soil around shrubs should be kept moist to some depth at all times.

Feeding

If the soil has been properly prepared and enriched with compost or manure, no further fertilization should be required until the following spring. Don't be tempted to pour on packaged plant food in the belief that your young shrubs will grow so much faster! They can only absorb a limited amount, and any extra chemical fertilizer added may increase the soil's salinity and possibly burn the roots of the young plants. If there is still no sign of growth three or four months after planting, you could apply complete plant food *then*, as directed on the packet. *Never* exceed the application rates, and *don't* fertilize any time from mid-autumn to the end of winter. Always water first, then fertilize and water again.

Pruning

Pruning is not the repetitious task it is so often thought to be; it rarely needs to be repeated more than once per year. But pruning improves the vigour of most shrubs and leads to better flower production.

Prune to preserve the shrub's natural habit while reducing its size. Do not shear evenly all over unless you are trying to force it to grow into an artificial shape, as in a topiary. As a general rule, prune after bloom.

Deciduous shrubs which flower in late winter or spring on shoots grown the previous season should be pruned as soon as the flowers have finished. Cut around 1/3 of the oldest stems completely away to make room for vigorous new growth. Shorten the remaining stems by about 1/3 also, cutting just above an outward-pointing bud. Shoots always grow in the same direction as the bud from which they spring, so prune to avoid a mass of criss-crossing stems in the centre of the bush.

Shrubs which flower later in spring, or in summer, on the same season's growth should be pruned in winter before growth commences.

Evergreen shrubs should not be pruned until all danger of frost damage has passed, though naturally that advice is only applicable in cold winter areas.

Regular pinching out of the growing tips encourages dense, twiggy growth and more bloom, and is recommended for young shrubs.

When you *do* prune, use only clean secateurs so as not to damage plant tissue. First remove any dead or broken branches and any part of the shrub badly infested with insects or fungus diseases. Remove one of each pair of crossing branches, being careful not to leave stubs which might form easy points of entry for pests or diseases. Cut them flush and dress with wound paint.

Very old or straggly shrubs can be revitalized by cutting every branch almost to the ground in earliest spring. Masses of new shoots will emerge and grow quickly into a dense plant. Clearly, such drastic pruning should not be undertaken very often.

Propagation

A well designed garden, bursting with colour and fragrance, will always attract admiration. Visitors will often express great interest when individual shrubs are looking at their best, and would be delighted to receive a healthy young plant as a memento.

Propagating your own shrubs is easy and rewarding. They make wonderful gifts, and if you are thinking of expanding the garden, producing your own shrubs can save a lot of money. Suggestions on propagation are included in the entry for each plant. Some plants are best multiplied by sowing seed, others by taking cuttings and divisions, or by making grafts or layers. Seeds take anything from a few days to many months to germinate, and the result may be a tiny seedling that is not large enough to plant out for three or four years. Seedlings, moreover, may not come true to type, especially if the parent is a hybrid. Such seedlings often lose all the features that distinguish the prized hybrid from a perfectly ordinary natural species. To be sure of getting an identical plant and of getting it as quickly as possible, vegetative propagation must be used—that is, propagating from parts of the original plant as detailed below.

Taking cuttings

Depending on the age of the material taken, cuttings are described as soft tip, semi-hardwood or hardwood.

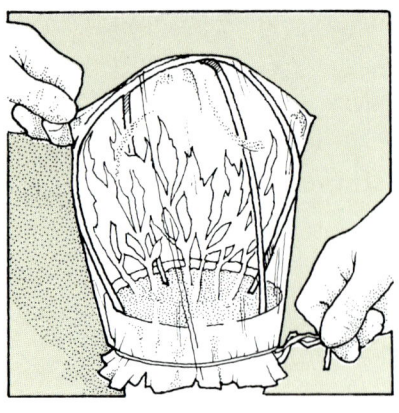

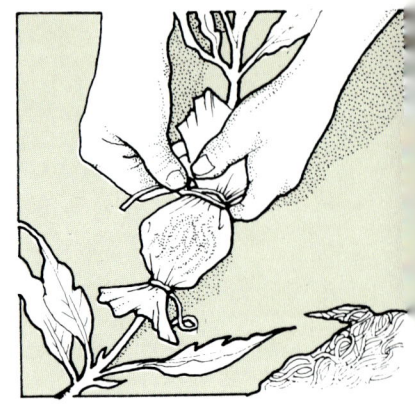

G: Soft tip-cuttings are struck in sand mixture, underneath plastic.

H: To layer, pin down a flexible cut branch, cover with soil.

I: Air-layer by wrapping cut twig in sphagnum, air-tight plastic.

Soft tip cuttings are taken in spring and early summer from the top 10cm of vigorous new growth. The stem will be bright green, and should snap when bent sharply. If it does not snap, the shoot is too sappy and will not root anyway.

Semi-hardwood cuttings are taken in summer when the first flush of growth is beginning to mature. The stem, 10-15cm from the tip, should be turning brown and woody, and will bend before breaking. Both types of cuttings should be taken in the morning when plants are firm and full of sap. They wilt easily, so it is important to pot them up right away. Have pots or trays of a damp 50/50 mix of coarse sand and moist peat moss ready before taking the cuttings.

Make the cut with a very sharp knife about 1cm below a leaf junction (node). Trim off all flowers or flower buds so that all energy is directed into rooting. Remove all leaves on the lower third and cut those remaining in halves to reduce water loss by transpiration. If desired, dip the cut ends in hormone rooting powder and shake off the excess. These powders promote the rapid development of roots and are formulated for either hard or softwood cuttings. Insert the cuttings into holes in the soil mix made with a pencil or knitting needle. Firm down and water gently. Place the pots of cuttings in a propagating box if you have one or enclose each one in a clear plastic bag. Insert sticks into the pots of cuttings to keep the plastic raised above the young plants. Set the cuttings in a bright but shaded spot and keep moist, never wet. Some soft tip or semi-hardwood cuttings take only 2-3 weeks to strike, while others may take months. New leaf growth signals success. Re-pot rooted cuttings individually, and grow on till big enough to plant out.

Hardwood cuttings are taken from deciduous shrubs in late autumn or winter, when all the leaves have dropped. Select only strong, healthy branches and, using sharp cutters, remove 60cm lengths. Cut these into 10-15cm sections with at least 4 buds on each section. The lower cut should be made 7cm below a node, and the top cut about 3cm above a node. Tie the cuttings together in a bundle with all the tops at one end, and note which *is* the top end. Put the bundle in a box on a layer of moist sand-peat mixture, lay it horizontally, and cover with about 15cm more of the mix. Cover the box and store in a cool but not freezing spot all winter. By spring, the cuttings should have developed roots, and can be potted up separately by burying each cutting so that only the top bud is exposed above soil. Grow on in sun until large enough to plant out, probably 2-3 seasons.

Dividing plants and making layers

Some shrubs reproduce themselves by forming suckers at a distance from the main plant. These suckers arise from the ends of underground stems and produce their own roots while still attached to the parent plant. By severing the underground stem with a sharp spade and carefully digging up the sucker, a new, relatively large plant can be had immediately. Make sure, though, that the sucker is from the plant you want, and not from a stock used previously in grafting.

If only one or two shrubs are needed, a method called layering produces good-sized plants over a period of six months to a year. Layering is easiest on

Hedge of Oleanders (*Nerium* sp.) in southern California

shrubs that form long, flexible canes from a central clump—*Forsythia* and *Kolkwitzia* for example. These flexible canes are staked down so that they touch the ground 30-45cm from their tips. The cane is nicked where it contacts the soil, the cut wedged open with a matchstick or similar and dusted with hormone rooting powder. The soil should be loosened and broken up so that it is fine and crumbly, and the stem held down with U-shaped pieces of coat-hanger wire. Once it's staked down, heap soil on top of the nicked section and water thoroughly. If this is done in spring (in temperate areas), the layer will probably have rooted and can be detached the following autumn. In cold countries, it is wiser to leave the layer till next spring.

The Japanese are past-masters at air-layering— a complicated process which makes it possible to root quite large pieces of growth on a shrub *without* flexible branches. In this, a tiny ring of bark is taken from right around the selected branch. This is dressed with rooting hormone, the whole covered with damp sphagnum moss and (in the modern version) the wound wrapped in clear plastic, which is tied tightly on each side of the dressing to prevent the escape of moisture. Roots form on the outer side of the wound, and the plastic is removed when they become visible through the mass of sphagnum moss. When the new roots become apparent, the branch is unwrapped and sawn through below them. The plant is then potted up; some support is needed until the new roots have grown sufficiently long to anchor the plant. It may also be advisable to keep the foliage covered to prevent moisture loss.

How to Use This Book

All flowering and fragrant shrubs included in this book are arranged in the alphabetical order of their botanical names, so you can just leaf through until you come to the plant you want. If you know only a popular name, e.g., Night Jessamine, turn to the comprehensive index beginning page 173. Here, the popular name entry will refer you to the shrub's botanical name, and the number of the page on which the entry begins, e.g., Night Jessamine, see *Cestrum* 43. There are more popular names listed than there are entries in the book because many shrubs have more than one popular name.

Altogether, more than 400 varieties of flowering shrubs are described. Over 335 are illustrated in colour. Each entry includes a great deal of useful information, some of it in abbreviated form in the heading. The first line of each entry gives the shrub's generic name only, in large capital letters. This may be followed by a synonym (when there is one by which the plant is sometimes sold), e.g.,

CESTRUM
(*syn HABROTHAMNUS*)

The Latin name is followed by one or more popular names in normal type. After this come three lines in capitals. The first line, e.g.,

SPRING–AUTUMN

indicates the seasons in which the shrub blooms. The second line, e.g.,

FAST/LONG SEASON

indicates first the shrub's speed of growth to flowering size, and following the oblique stroke the length of blooming season, generally short or long, sometimes all year. The third line, e.g.,

HT: TO 150cm/5ft

indicates the plant's maximum height under ideal growing conditions; this will help you decide where to plant. It will also suggest whether the shrub may need staking, as in fact almost any plant over 75cm/ 2½ ft tall will, at least initially. Sometimes, where several species are covered in the one entry, the height will be expressed in the form of a range: e.g.,

HT: 60-180cm/2-6ft

In such cases, comparative heights of individual species may be described in the entry itself. This line

could also include an additional word or two e.g., ERECT, ARCHING CANES, when the plant's growth is exceptional in some way.

Finally, each heading includes a group of symbols, one or more in the form of a rayed sun, others as letters enclosed by squares.

☼   indicates the shrub does best in full sun. These are good as specimens.

◑   shows the shrub prefers sun for only part of a day. These could be ideal on east or west side of your home.

✸   (the rarest) shows the plant will flower in full shade. Ideal for use among trees.

C   shows that the shrub blooms well in cold-winter areas (but it may also grow elsewhere).

T   that it flowers in temperate climates (though range may be wider).

H   that the plant does well in tropics. Few cold-climate plants bloom in the tropics as well.

As some shrubs are quite adaptable, the symbols may appear in many different combinations, as where a plant will grow in both cold and temperate climates, will bloom in full sun or part shade.

Information within the entry itself details methods and seasons of propagation, which may vary widely from plant to plant. Pruning times and techniques are also noted, together with the amount of water and fertilization needed; whether the shrub is frost hardy; whether it will grow in desert or seaside conditions. Countries of origin are noted, the type of soil preferred and also whether the shrub is deciduous or evergreen. Often these notes will include information on special planting positions— for instance if the plant makes good ground cover, or can be sheared as a hedge, whether it can be used in containers, or is useful in damp soil.

Finally, a note on the book's title. All shrubs must flower, but we confine ourselves in this book to those grown specifically for their floral display. Fragrance is more subjective. What smells nice to you may not to me, but many of the included shrubs are universally appreciated for their fragrance, and this too is noted in the heading, in red type.

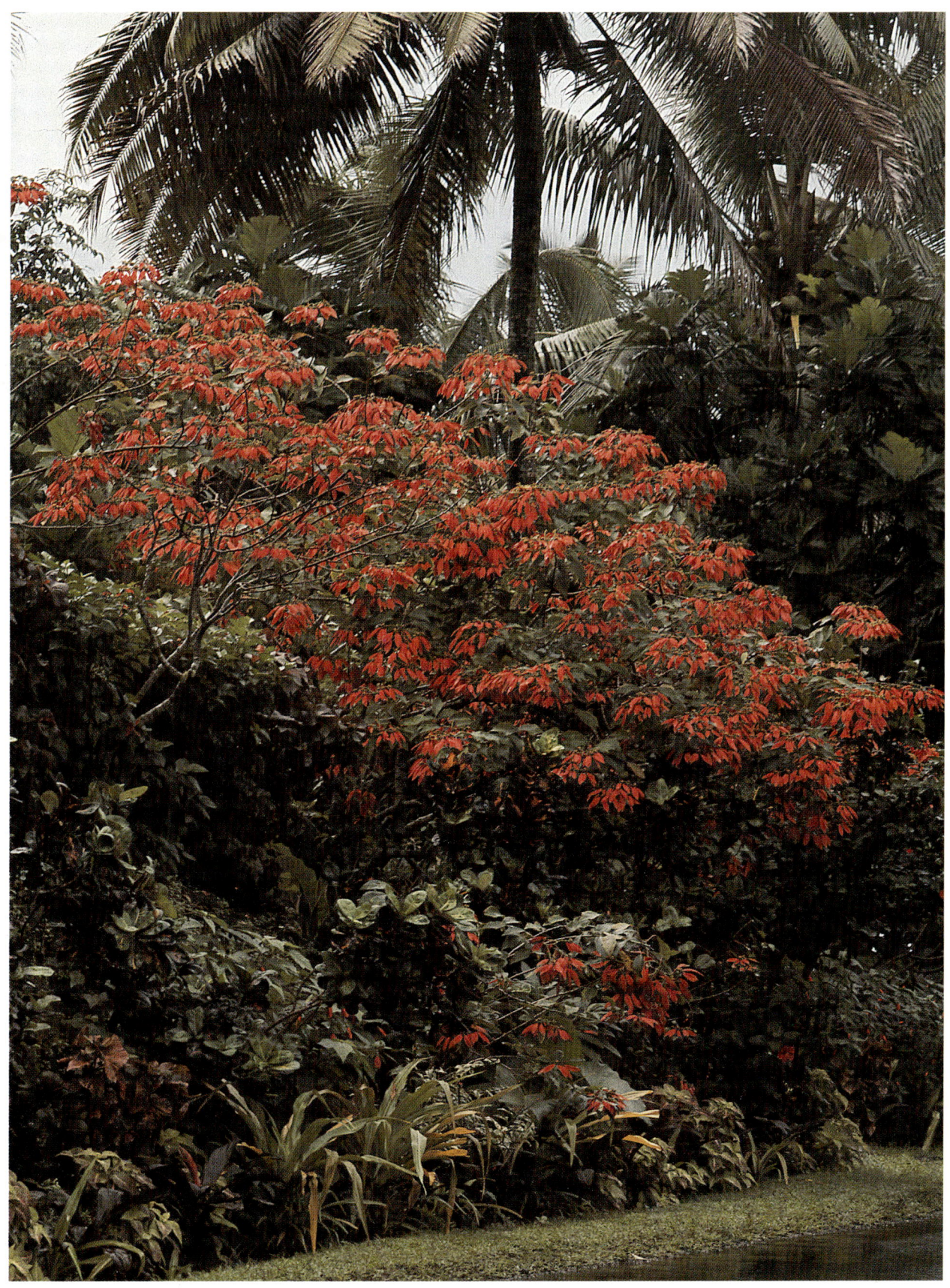

Among the most gorgeous of tropical shrubs, these
Poinsettias were planted beside the road in American
Samoa.

ABELIA

Abelia

☼ ☀
C T

SUMMER–AUTUMN
FAST/LONG DISPLAY
HT: 1-2m/3-6ft/SPREADING

Panicles of dainty bell-flowers clustered at the tips of graceful, arching canes are the hallmark of *Abelia*, a useful shrub genus from China and Mexico. Lightly toothed, glossy foliage, a fountain-like habit and persistent red calyces are other decorative features. All species may be planted out in autumn or early spring in any leaf-rich soil; they prefer full sun. In really cold areas, they'll need the shelter of a wall or larger bushes to protect from prevailing winds. Popular species include: Mexican *A. floribunda* with tubular carmine blooms 4.5cm long: *A.* X *grandiflora* with pink-flushed bells only 1.5cm long. Its variegated sport *tricolor* is most attractive. Chinese *A. schumannii* has a denser habit, 2.5cm mauve-pink blooms. All normally deciduous, they'll remain evergreen in warmer climates. Propagate from summer cuttings at a temperature of 16°C/61°F. Prune to change habit in winter, trim lightly from time to time where a more compact shape is desired. Feed in spring.

ABELIA X *grandiflora tricolor*
Variegated Abelia

ABELIA schumannii
Schumann's Abelia

ABUTILON

Flowering Maple,
Chinese Lantern,
Chinese Bellflower

☼ ☀
T H

SPRING–AUTUMN
FAST/LONG DISPLAY
HT: 1.5-2.5m/4½-8ft/OFTEN TRAILING

Untidy, leggy shrubs for the most part, *Abutilons* are best trained up columns or against sunny walls so the beauty of their hanging flowers can be enjoyed all through the warm weather. They like a position with rich, damp soil, but flower best in full sun, so a compromise is often necessary. Pinch back often to encourage branching and improved flower yield. Heavy feeding makes them bolt, so give only a very dilute fertilizer to replace nutrient leached out of the soil by heavy summer watering. Most commonly seen are the many garden-raised cultivars grouped as *A. X hybridum*. These include 'Emperor' and 'Vesuvius' with red flowers, pink 'Tunisia', bright yellow 'Golden Fleece' and white 'Boule de Neige'. All have variably toothed heart-shaped leaves with a furry texture and flowers borne at the leaf axils. *Abutilons* can be raised from seed sown any time and kept at a temperature of 24°C/75°F. They'll germinate in 3 weeks or less, and should flower within 12 months, but named varieties must be propagated from cuttings. These may be taken from old wood in warmer weather or as firm new tips late in the season. Strike indoors under heat in a peat/sand mixture. Some 100 natural species of these striking plants are also grown. Among the most worthwhile is the sprawling 'Big River Abutilon', *A. megapotamicum* from Brazil, particularly in its variegated form. This may be used as a dense groundcover in warmer areas, or trained as a wall-shrub. Sometimes it even decides to climb by itself! Its narrow-ovate leaves are lightly toothed and variegated with yellow blotches. The pendant, tubular flowers rather resemble Fuchsias, but in red and yellow. Its hybrid *A. X milleri* has larger leaves and more open, red-veined blooms. *A. pictum* has deeply-lobed, maple-like leaves of a smooth texture, with orange blooms veined in red. Its variegated form 'Souvenir de Bonn' is illustrated. In cold climates *Abutilons* are often raised as indoor plants; bloom best when rootbound.

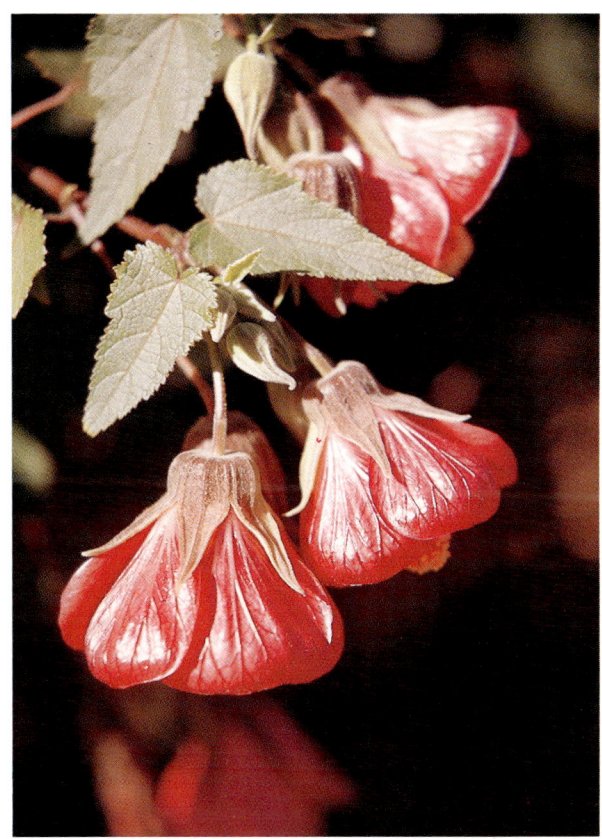

ABUTILON X hybridum 'Emperor'
Chinese Bellflower

ABUTILON X milleri
Hybrid Bellflower

ABUTILON pictum 'Souvenir de Bonn'
Flowering Maple

ABUTILON megapotamicum
Big River Abutilon

ACOKANTHERA FRAGRANT

Wintersweet,
Bushman's Poison

☼
T H

SPRING
SLOW/LONG DISPLAY
HT: TO 3m/10ft/WIDE

In the days before civilization came to Africa, this genus of decorative shrubs was valued principally as the source of an arrow poison. But white settlers eagerly adopted them for garden use, particularly in coastal areas, for *Acokantheras* are tolerant of poor soil, wind and salt air. Plant in full sun as specimens, or trim as a hedge. All they need is ample water in summer to turn on a year-round show. In the case of *A. oblongifolia,* the evergreen 12.5cm leaves glow with red-purple, and dense clusters of pale pink flowers appear all year. They are lightly fragrant, and followed by 2.5cm plum-coloured poisonous fruits in autumn and winter. Propagate from seeds, cuttings, or, in the case of the variegated form, by grafting. *Acokanthera* should be pruned lightly after bloom, is hardy down to −2°C/28°F.

ACOKANTHERA oblongifolia variegata
Bushman's Poison

ACTINODIUM

Swamp Daisy,
Albany Daisy

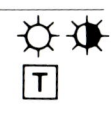

WINTER–SPRING
SLOW/SHORT DISPLAY
HT: 1m/3ft

Papery pink and white daisy-flowers nod on thin stems of *Actinodium*, the Swamp Daisy, a useful shrub for acid coastal soils. Raise from cuttings, which strike easily in a damp mixture of peat and sand. Then grow where they'll receive full sun all year but get wet feet during the cool-weather flowering period. An erect, brittle plant with heath-like foliage, *Actinodium cunninghamii* is altogether sparsely furnished when not in bloom. Though its spring flowers look like daisies (Asteraceae), they actually belong to the same family as eucalypts (Myrtaceae). The flower stems can be dried for arrangements, but the pale blooms are sometimes coloured by standing stems in a dye/water mixture. Short lived, *Actinodium* may be pruned in spring.

ACTINODIUM cunninghamii
Swamp Daisy

ADENIUM

Desert Rose,
Desert Azalea,
Impala Lily,
Sabie Star

WINTER–SPRING
SLOW/LONG DISPLAY
HT: TO 2m/6ft IN CULTIVATION

Named for the former British colony of Aden, part of its natural territory, the gorgeously flowering Desert Rose (*Adenium obesum*) resembles and is closely related to the Frangipani. A tall, sparsely branched shrub in nature, with a swollen trunk base, it is more often seen in cultivation as a rather dwarfed pot plant. More drought resistant than Frangipani, it is propagated from dried-off branches struck in damp sand. *Adeniums* are evergreen in a warm climate, but it is useless to try them where there is frost. The leaves are glossy; oval but widest at the tips. Flowers are a brilliant scarlet-pink, centred with white and yellow, and borne in terminal clusters. They like a dry winter, good drainage.

ADENIUM obesum
Desert Rose

AGAPETES serpens
Flame Heath

AGAPETES
(syn *PENTAPTERYGIUM*)

Flame Heath

WINTER–SUMMER
SLOW/LONG DISPLAY
HT: TO 1.5m/5ft/ARCHING BRANCHES

Though many species of this interesting genus grow wild in Asia, only one is in cultivation: the flame heath, *Agapetes serpens*, a decorative plant known for many years as Pentapterygium, and often sold under that name. Usually rather squat, it grows from a tuberous rootstock and sends out slender, weeping branches that are densely hairy and furnished with evergreen 1cm red-tipped leaves. The tubular flowers of vivid scarlet may appear any time from winter on, hanging loosely in pairs beneath the arching stems and sometimes bending them with their weight. *Agapetes* are propagated from tip cuttings which strike easily in summer and autumn in a sand/peat mixture, or at other times in a glasshouse with mist and bottom heat. Sometimes epiphytic in nature, these decorative shrubs demand perfect drainage; most effective as a container plant or set in a large rockery. *Agapetes* enjoy leafy, acid soil, plenty of water, and a light feeding with organic manure in autumn. They revel in partly shaded conditions with high humidity. Tip prune regularly to encourage a dense, compact shape.

ALLAMANDA FRAGRANT

Golden Trumpet Bush,
Bush Allamanda

SUMMER
AVERAGE/LONG DISPLAY
HT: 1-2m/3-6ft

☀ T H

Showy-flowered plants from South America, *Allamandas* mostly climb and sprawl untidily, are used in the tropics for informal fences. One species, however, *A. neriifolia,* is content to remain as a shrub, and can make a spectacular specimen in a sunny courtyard in temperate climates. Propagated from 8cm tip cuttings taken in spring, it grows into a compact bush in well-drained soil. Light watering is sufficient in colder weather, but in the warmer months it should be stepped up and alternated with liquid manure to produce dazzling clusters of 6cm golden trumpet flowers. *Allamanda* may drop a few leaves in cooler areas, where it can be used as a greenhouse specimen. A minimum winter temperature of 10°C/50°F is required. Prune heavily.

ALLAMANDA neriifolia
Golden Trumpet Bush

ALYOGYNE
(syn *HIBISCUS*)

Blue Hibiscus

SPRING–SUMMER
VERY FAST/LONG DISPLAY
HT: 2m/6ft

☀ ☀ T

A stunning Hibiscus-lookalike from southwest Australia, *Alyogyne huegelii* is also widely grown in California and other temperate areas. It will withstand a light frost without problems, and will flourish in quite a range of soils. Easily propagated from seed, or from cuttings taken any time and struck in a fast-draining mixture of peat and sand, *Alyogyne* is a rather scraggy bush of open, spreading habit. Its rough stems are lightly clothed with 8cm leaves, generally 5-lobed and hairy, with each lobe deeply toothed. The showy warm-weather blossoms are up to 15cm in diameter, their shiny overlapping petals twisted like the blades of a ship's propellor. Somewhat brittle, *Alyogyne* needs wind protection.

ALYOGYNE huegelii
Blue Hibiscus

APHELANDRA

Zebra Plant and others

SUMMER–AUTUMN
AVERAGE/SHORT DISPLAY
HT: 25-450cm/1-15ft

One of the more spectacular South American shrub genera, *Aphelandras* are familiar as indoor plants, for a minimum winter temperature of 10°C/50°F is a must if they are to survive. But in warm climates with rich porous soil they turn on a magnificent summer show outdoors. *Aphelandras* are members of the acanthus family, with typical spear-shaped leaves and terminal spikes of showy, tubular flowers. Given the right climatic conditions, they are easy to grow from cuttings and self-seed readily in tropical gardens. All species need dilute fertilizer and plenty of water while in active growth, tapering off the supply after bloom, when the entire flower head will drop away. To avoid legginess, prune hard after flowering in earliest spring. *A. X louisae* grows to 30cm: *A. aurantiaca* to 100cm: *A. sinclaireana* to 450cm in the tropics but much less in mild climates.

APHELANDRA aurantiaca

APHELANDRA sinclaireana

APHELANDRA X louisae
Zebra Plant

ARCTOSTAPHYLOS

Manzanita,
Bearberry

SPRING
AVERAGE/LONG DISPLAY
HT: 1-1.5m/3-4½ft/SPRAWLING

When the first European botanists in California enquired the uses of the plants they saw, local Indians told them that one particular genus of shrubs was a great attraction to grizzly bears. So the botanists called the plants *Arctostaphylos*, from two Greek words meaning 'bear-grape'. Confined to western areas of North and Central America, they are mostly low, spreading bushes with reddish stems and small, leathery leaves that are almost hidden in spring beneath a profusion of bloom. All 50-odd species are easy to grow from seed, autumn cuttings or by separation of self-layered branches which are easy to locate. Light watering and feeding are required, with regular pinching and pruning to control the sprawling habit.

ARCTOSTAPHYLOS densiflora
Bear Berry, Manzanita

ASTARTEA
(*syn* BAECKEA)

(no popular name)

ALL YEAR
AVERAGE/INTERMITTENT DISPLAY
HT: 1m/3ft/SPREADING

Producing a never-ending display of bloom once established, the genus *Astartea* was named for a Phoenician goddess of fertility who was equally generous with her favours. Like many Australian plants, the *Astarteas* belong to the myrtle family, and dislike extreme humidity. They are highly adaptable, tolerating frost, salt air, drought and even water-logged soil. They have minimal need of water or nutriment, and pruning is needed only to keep the bushes compact. Illustrated *Astartea fascicularis* can be grown from tip-cuttings taken any time, or from ripe seed sown thinly on a sieved sand/peat mixture. The typical 5-petalled myrtle flowers are about 1cm in diameter and may be white or rose pink. The needle-leaves are evergreen.

ASTARTEA fascicularis

AZALEA
(syn RHODODENDRON) SOME FRAGRANT

(no other popular name)

SPRING–AUTUMN
AVERAGE/INTERMITTENT DISPLAY [C] [T]
HT: 30-350cm/1-10ft/SPREADING

It may come as a shock to discover there is no such plant as an *Azalea*—at least not so far as botanists and taxonomists are concerned. All species were reclassified under *Rhododendron* long, long ago. But experience has taught that the home gardener is very stubborn in the matter of such a major name change. Azaleas they were, Azaleas they are, and Azaleas they will always be, one suspects. Though both groups (Azaleas and *Rhododendrons*) are relative newcomers on the garden scene, there did at one time seem to be sufficient difference between them to warrant separate classification. Last century, *Rhododendrons* were thought of as large evergreen plants whose blooms included 10 stamens, while Azaleas were much smaller shrubs with only five stamens per flower and mostly with deciduous leaves. But in the early years of the 20th century, botanical explorers returned with masses of new *Rhododendron* species, and suddenly the distinction became quite blurred.

The Azaleas we grow today are cross-bred from literally dozens of original species. As a general rule, what we call *Azalea indica* species are descendants of *Rhododendron simsii*; the Kurume Azaleas descend from *R. obtusum*; the Mollis Azaleas from *R. japonicum*; and the Korean Azaleas from *R. yedoense*. The evergreen Indicas and Kurumes are most commonly grown in warmer climates, the deciduous Mollis and related Ghent and Exbury hybrids where winters are cold. Late-blooming cold resistant *A. macrantha* hybrids are popular in both climates. Indica Azaleas bloom mostly in shades of pink, mauve and white, and may grow to 3m in both height and width. A subdivision, the Belgian hybrid Indicas, include many double blooms, rich red tones, and rarely exceed 1m in height. These are very popular as pot subjects.

The small Kurume Azaleas have daintier blooms and leaves, and are most often seen either in rockeries or mass-planted as groundcovers. Some

varieties grow only 60cm in height and more than most Azaleas, they flower in both spring and autumn. Gumpo Azaleas, a division of the Macranthas, are also evergreen, have large flowers, but rarely grow above 25cm. The Mollis, Ghent and Exbury hybrid Azaleas are deciduous, and often perfumed. They include many unusual shades of cream, beige, green, apricot, orange, yellow and flame.

All Azaleas are surface rooters and can be moved satisfactorily even in bloom. They should not be planted too deeply or mulched heavily lest older,

AZALEA macrantha rosea
Satsuki Azalea

deeper roots rot and the plant die.

An acid soil with a pH of 5 to 6 is ideal, preferably light, leafy and well-drained. Alkaline soil, or the addition of lime, is almost always fatal. Most species can be grown from 5cm cuttings taken in summer or autumn and struck under glass in a mixture of peat and sand. Larger plants can be layered in mid-spring; layers lifted late autumn. Pruning is not essential but advisable if plants are not to become too leggy. Bloom is more profuse when they are kept compact by shearing.

In some countries, a fungal infection known as petal blight is a problem. Where this is so, the entire plant must be sprayed with a recommended fungicide at fortnightly intervals, over and under the foliage. This should commence at first colour of flower buds. Also, the Azalea plants should be watered from that time only by dribbling around the roots, not by overhead spraying, which helps spread the blight.

Azalea lacefly and thrip are a problem in some areas, but can be controlled by spraying under the foliage in warm weather with a systemic insecticide.

AZALEA X '*Narcissiflora*'
a Ghent Hybrid Azalea

AZALEA X '*Red Ruby*'
a Kurume Azalea

AZALEA X 'Alba Magna'
an Indica Azalea

AZALEA X 'Alphonse Anderson'
an Indica Azalea

Azalea pontica

AZALEA X *'Gibraltar'*
a Mollis Azalea

AZALEA X *'Elsa Karga'*
a Belgian Hybrid Azalea

AZALEA X *'Coccinea Speciosa'*
a Ghent Hybrid Azalea

BANKSIA

Banksia,
Honeysuckle

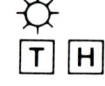

SPRING–AUTUMN
SLOW/LONG DISPLAY
HT: 3m/10ft/SPREADING

As endemic to Australia as *Proteas* are to South Africa, the *Banksias* were named for Cook's fellow explorer, Sir Joseph Banks. There are almost 50 species, all enjoying a warm position in sandy, acid soil, enriched with leaf-mould. Shrubby species may be propagated from seed or tip-cuttings, can be planted any time of the year, are mostly slow growing. Illustrated *B. baxteri*, the Bird's Nest Banksia, is unique in its leathery, zig-zag foliage, reddish bark and gorgeous compound flowers which open from greenish-white to a rich gold as the stamens are exserted from hundreds of tubular flowerets. It is drought-tolerant and useful in protected coastal gardens. The inflorescence will last for years in permanent arrangements.

BANKSIA baxteri
Bird's Nest Banksia

BARLERIA

Philippine Violet

SUMMER
AVERAGE/LONG DISPLAY
HT: 1m/3ft/DENSE

Neither a violet, nor from the Philippines if the truth be known, this charming evergreen shrub will need winter protection under glass where the temperature drops below 13°C/55°F. *Barleria cristata* makes a spectacular tub plant for the sunny terrace, and is often seen trimmed into a hedge in the tropics. It can be propagated either by seed or from half-ripened cuttings struck in a sharp, moist rooting medium at any time apart from winter. *Barleria* enjoys summer humidity, dry winters and an acid soil rich in leaf-mould and manure. Give it plenty of water all summer long and light shade protection if possible, as the minutely hairy foliage is inclined to scorch in direct sun. Both white and mauve flowered varieties are available.

BARLERIA cristata
Philippine Violet

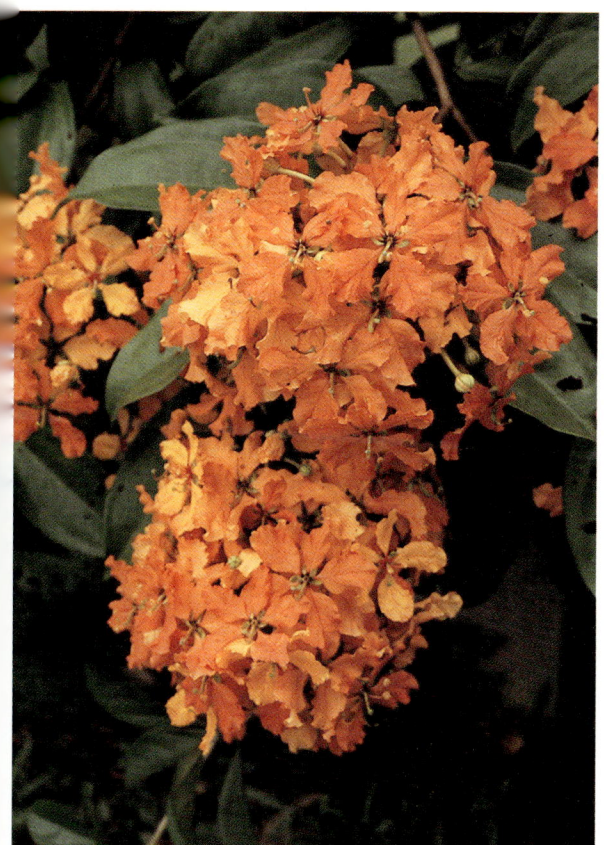

BAUHINIA

South African Orchid Bush,
Pride of de Kaap

SPRING–AUTUMN
FAST/LONG DISPLAY
HT: 2-3m/7-10ft/SPREADING

Showiest members of the pea family, *Bauhinias* are magnificent when well grown, their branches often covered in orchid-like flowers. They grow readily from seed or cuttings, will thrive with protection in any climate down to a winter minimum of 7°C/45°F. The genus is scattered from southern Africa up through India and Southeast Asia and down again to Australia. Most commonly seen are the Asiatic tree species which flower on bare wood in early spring— even winter in a warm climate. But the illustrated shrubby species bloom later in the year, well after the curious twin-lobed foliage has developed. They make spectacular groundcover or wall shrubs, should be cut back hard immediately after bloom.

BAUHINIA kockiana
Nasturtium Bauhinia

BAUHINIA galpinii
South African Orchid Bush

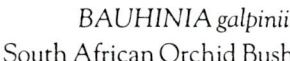

BEAUFORTIA

Swamp Bottlebrush,
Gravel Bottlebrush

☼

SUMMER–AUTUMN
AVERAGE/LONG DISPLAY
HT: 2-4m/6-14ft/ERECT TO SPREADING

T H

Named for Mary, Duchess of Beaufort, an early 19th century patron of botany, *Beaufortias* form yet another spectacular West Australian genus of the myrtle family, generally with tiny, stem-clasping leaves and bright scarlet flowers arranged in brush-like spikes. Illustrated *Beaufortia sparsa* will grow in a variety of conditions from a temperate climate right into the subtropics. Often found in swampy areas, it will also flourish in seaside gardens, even hot, dry areas. It is raised from cuttings of half-ripe shoots, or seed from the previous year's capsules. These should be stored in a warm place until they open, and the seed scattered on a damp sand/peat mixture, hardly covered. Prune lightly after bloom.

BEAUFORTIA sparsa
Swamp Bottlebrush

BERBERIS

Barberry

☼

SPRING–AUTUMN
FAST/LONG DISPLAY
HT: 2-3m/6-10ft/BUSHY

C T

Almost 500 species of these colourful cool-climate shrubs have been recorded, from the northern and southern hemispheres. There are both deciduous and evergreen types, generally bearing sharp spines, gay yellow flowers in spring and attractive fruit in autumn. Deciduous species are good in cooler districts where autumn colours develop. Shown *Berberis darwinii* however is an evergreen South American type with small, shining holly-like leaves, and racemes of golden flowers that bear an extra-ordinary resemblance to tiny daffodils. The succeeding blue berries last into autumn. *Berberis* likes rich, well-drained soil, heavy watering only in a dry summer. It may be grown from autumn seed or cuttings from lateral shoots with a heel in late summer. Prune lightly after flowering to shape.

BERBERIS darwinii
Darwin Barberry

BORONIA

Boronia

SPRING
FAST/SHORT DISPLAY
HT: 30-150cm/1-5ft/ERECT

These dainty Australian shrubs include almost 70 species, but are difficult to grow away from their natural bushland. They need sandy, acid soil that drains fast, yet is so rich in humus it never dries out. All have slender leaves with three leaflets and tiny flowers which vary from lantern-shaped to fully open. They should be struck from firm tip-cuttings in coarse sand, as seed germination is highly erratic. The best known species is short-lived brown and chartreuse *Boronia megastigma*, which exudes an unforgettable perfume in spring. Rosy-red flowered *B. heterophylla* is popular in the cut flower trade. Both make good container plants, and benefit from a very light pruning of recently-flowered shoots. This helps keep them compact and has been shown to extend their life span.

BORONIA heterophylla
Kalgan Boronia

BORONIA megastigma
Brown Boronia

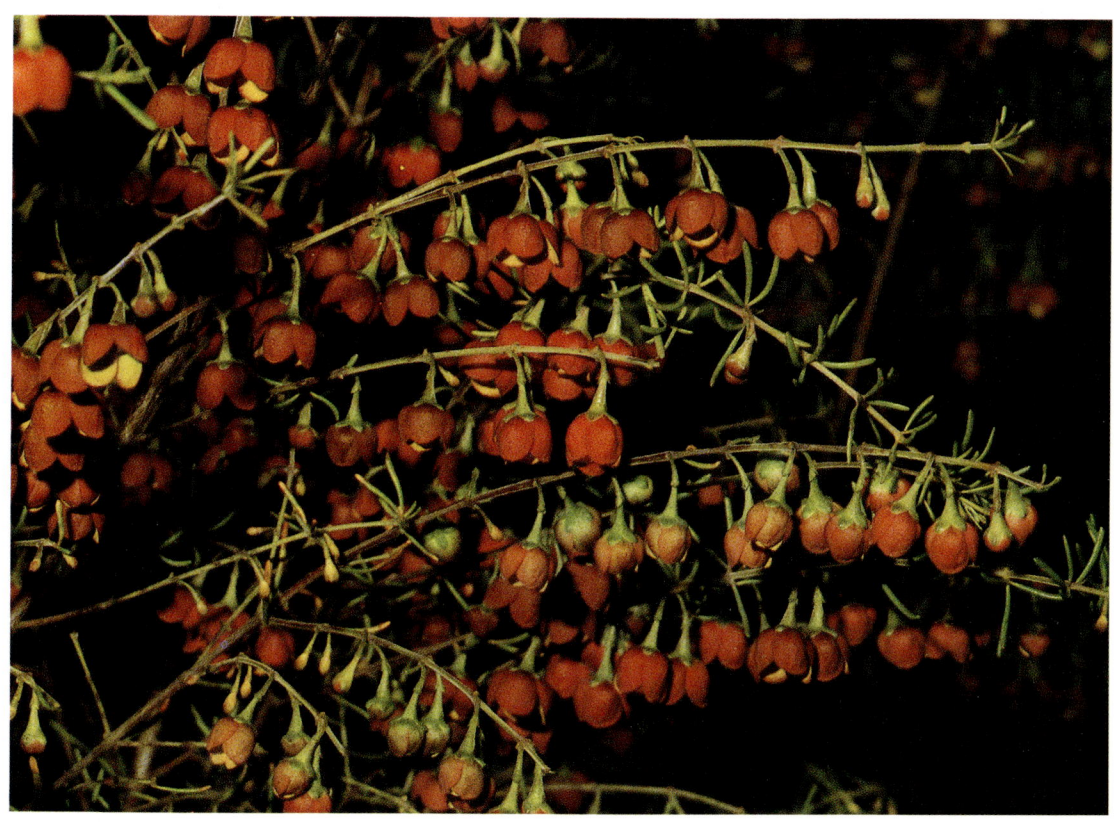

BOUVARDIA SOME FRAGRANT

Scented Bouvardia

AUTUMN–SPRING
AVERAGE/LONG DISPLAY
HT: 1m/3ft/UNTIDY

☼ T H

Often misunderstood, *Bouvardias* are really easy to grow in sheltered places with good soil. Just remember they cannot stand frosts—and will always be untidy unless you cut them almost to the ground after flowering and pinch back regularly. Whatever you do, only the white species, *Bouvardia humboldtii* (syn *B. longiflora*), will ever develop that sweet perfume. A straggling, evergreen shrub with small, spear-shaped leaves, it enjoys a rich, well-drained loam, heavy watering in summer and dilute liquid fertilizer during flowering. Hardy down to 7°C/45°F, it may be propagated from 8cm spring cuttings. Keep *Bouvardia* shaded and water from below. The coloured species, hybrids of scentless *B. ternifolia*, may be single or double.

BOUVARDIA humboldtii
Humboldt Bouvardia

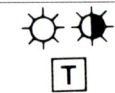

BRACHYSEMA lanceolata
Swan River Pea

BRACHYSEMA

Swan River Pea,
Scimitar Shrub

☼ ☀ T

ALL YEAR
AVERAGE
HT: 1m/3ft/SPREADING

An interesting member of the pea family from Western Australia, *Brachysema lanceolata* can only be preserved as a neat specimen by regular shaping after each burst of bloom. Otherwise it flops, and will only look good drooping over a wall, or sprawling on banks under light tree cover. It can also be turned into a semi-climber by tucking the young shoots into a panel of chicken wire. *Brachysema* prefers well-drained soil, but will withstand some waterlogging. Grow it from soft autumn tip-cuttings or seed scarified or soaked in hot water for 12 hours before sowing. The Swan River Pea grows well in California, and is hardy down to −5°C/23°F. Between blooming spurts, the foliage remains decorative, with lightly curled tips.

BRUNFELSIA

Brazil Raintree,
Yesterday Today and Tomorrow
Morning Noon and Night

SPRING–SUMMER
AVERAGE/LONG DISPLAY
HT: TO 3m/10ft IN CULTIVATION

Handsome evergreen shrubs for the frost-free garden, most *Brunfelsias* take on a multi-coloured appearance in spring and summer. The fragrant flowers, which open violet, fade to pale blue and finally white on successive days. There are some 30 species with this curious habit, all from South America and mostly resembling one another except in the size and profusion of the flowers. From the nearby West Indies another group, noted for their night fragrance, bloom in shades of white, green and pale butterscotch like the illustrated *B. americana* or Dama de Noche. All *Brunfelsias* enjoy rich, well-drained soil and heavy water in summer. Strike cuttings at 21°C/70°F. Prune only for shaping.

BRUNFELSIA pauciflora
Yesterday, Today & Tomorrow

BRUNFELSIA americana
Lady of the Night

BUDDLEIA FRAGRANT

Butterfly Bush,
Summer Lilac

☼

C T

SUMMER–AUTUMN
FAST/LONG DISPLAY
HT: TO 3m/10ft/ARCHING GROWTH

Evergreen in warm climates, deciduous in cold, the vigorous *Buddleias* or Butterfly Bushes need only water and good drainage to grow like weeds. The fragrant spikes of tiny gold-throated flowers (white, purple, crimson or orange according to variety) appear at various times from late winter. Leaves are pointed, crepe-textured and quite large (up to 30cm in illustrated *B. davidii* from China). Heavy watering is needed in the flowering months and the arching branches must be shortened to old wood after bloom. A light tip-pruning in spring will force laterals to bloom. Propagate from soft tip-cuttings in spring and summer, or semi-hard ones in autumn. The spicily fragrant blooms really do attract butterflies from far and wide.

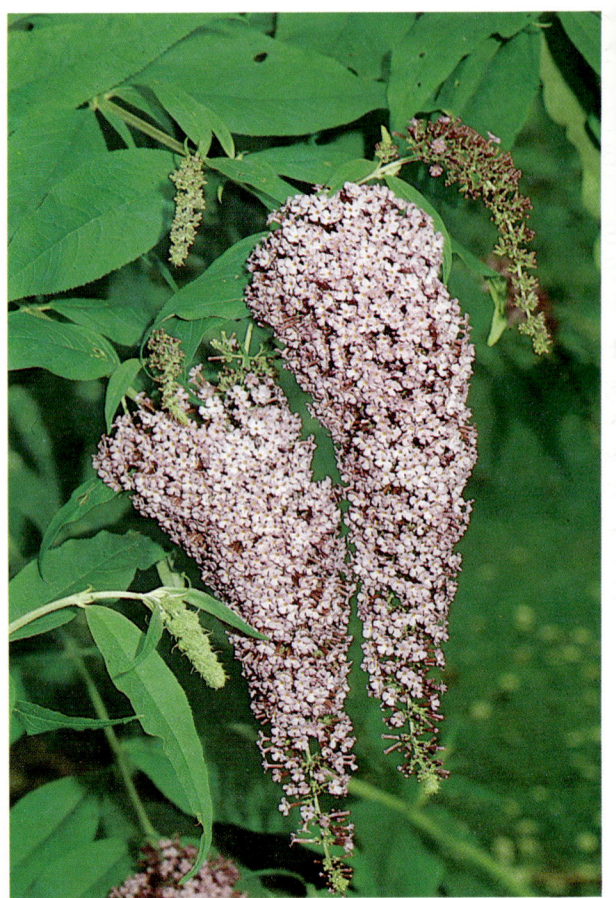

BUDDLEIA davidii
Butterfly Bush

BURCHELLIA   FRAGRANT

Buffalo Horn,
Wild Pomegranate,
Wildegranaat

☼ ☀

T

SPRING–SUMMER
AVERAGE/LONG DISPLAY
HT: TO 3m/10ft/BROAD

Not very common away from South Africa, the showy Wild Pomegranate is related to the Gardenia, and should be more widely grown. It is hardy down to −2°C/28°F, will grow easily where the soil is well-drained and enriched with compost. Raise from semi-hardwood cuttings taken in late summer or autumn and kept warm and humid until well-rooted. *Burchellia* may also be raised from seed sown in late winter, but does not always flower true to colour. The glossy evergreen foliage is exactly like that of a Gardenia, the showy orange-scarlet flowers open at branch-tips only. They are quite fragrant. There is only one species, known variously as *B. bubalina* or *B. capensis*. Shape after flowering.

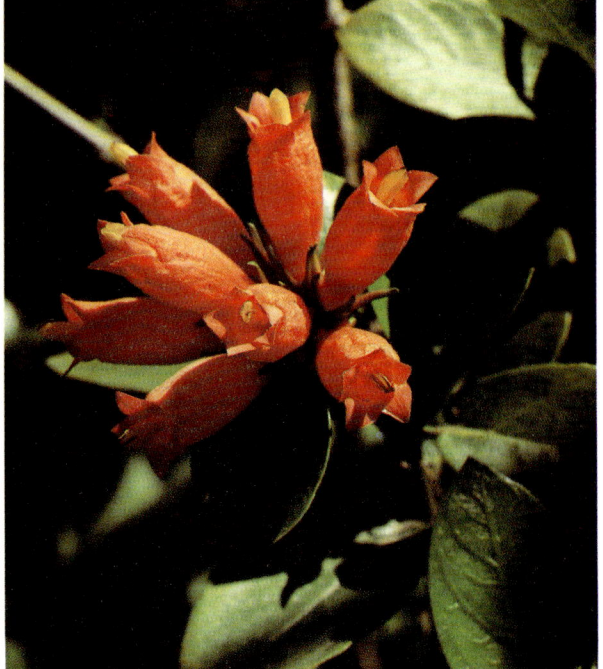

BURCHELLIA bubalina
Wildegranaat

CAESALPINIA

Dwarf Poinciana,
Bird of Paradise Bush

SUMMER
FAST/LONG DISPLAY
HT: 3m/10ft

Better known for its gorgeously flowering tree species, the genus *Caesalpinia* includes several handsome shrubs for warmer climates. The most often seen of these is illustrated *C. gilliesii*, a rather sparsely branched semi-deciduous plant that is sometimes used for bedding in the tropics. It also makes a handsome wall-shrub, with 20cm bipinnate leaves (remarkably like those of a Jacaranda) and terminal racemes up to 30cm and more long, bearing up to 40 yellow-petalled blooms, each centred with arching scarlet stamens. The shrub does best in well-drained, leaf-rich soil with light but regular water, and is most easily grown from seed. This should be soaked in warm water before sowing. Semi-hardwood tip-cuttings can also be struck with heat in a very sandy mixture with high humidity.

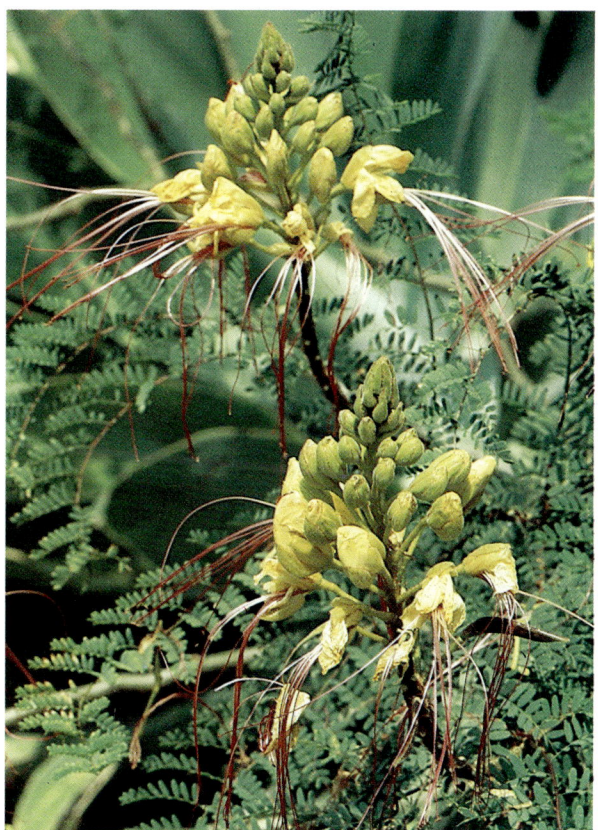

CAESALPINIA gilliesii
Dwarf Poinciana

CALLIANDRA

Powder Puff,
Tassel Flower,
Lehua Haole

AUTUMN–WINTER
FAST/LONG DISPLAY
HT: TO 3m/10ft/SPREADING

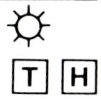

From South America, these really spectacular relatives of the Acacias are aptly named from the Greek *Kallos* (beauty) and *andros* (stamens), for their 7.5cm blooms are quite without petals. There are some 150 species, mostly with pink or white powder-puff flowers, but the loveliest is undoubtedly Bolivia's *Calliandra haematocephala*, the blood-red Tassel Flower. Every leaf is compounded of 2 stems, bearing up to 10 pairs of leaflets each, and the showy blooms appear at leaf axils throughout warm weather. *Calliandra* enjoys light soil with heavy summer water, and should be pruned in late winter for more compact growth. Propagate from ripe seed in spring, provided it can be kept moist and warm.

CALLIANDRA haematocephala
Red Powder Puff

CALLISTEMON

Bottlebrush

SPRING–AUTUMN
FAST/LONG DISPLAY
HT: 1.5-2m/5-7ft/UPRIGHT TO SPREADING

Evergreen shrubs and small trees from Australia which have become popular in frost-free areas throughout the world, *Callistemons* are often somewhat weeping in habit, their branches tipped in season with exciting brush-like flowers of red, pink, white, green or purple. From the ends of these, new leaves grow, by-passing a patch of woody seed-capsules which persist for years. Leaves vary from needle-like to spear-shaped with a silken, hairy texture—young foliage often tinted red or pink. All prefer a light, deep soil that is well drained but damp, and are found naturally on banks of streams. They may be propagated from spring seed, or from short, leafy tips taken in autumn and struck in a humid, misty atmosphere. Most tolerate frost and wind, the species C. *montanus* being suited to mountain gardens and cooler areas.

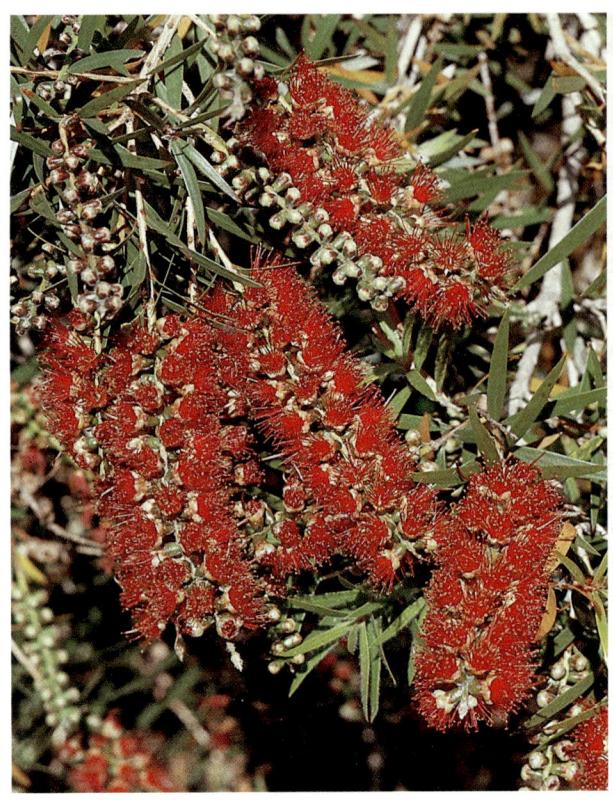

CALLISTEMON X 'Captain Cook'
Dwarf Bottlebrush

CALLISTEMON montanus
Mountain Bottlebrush

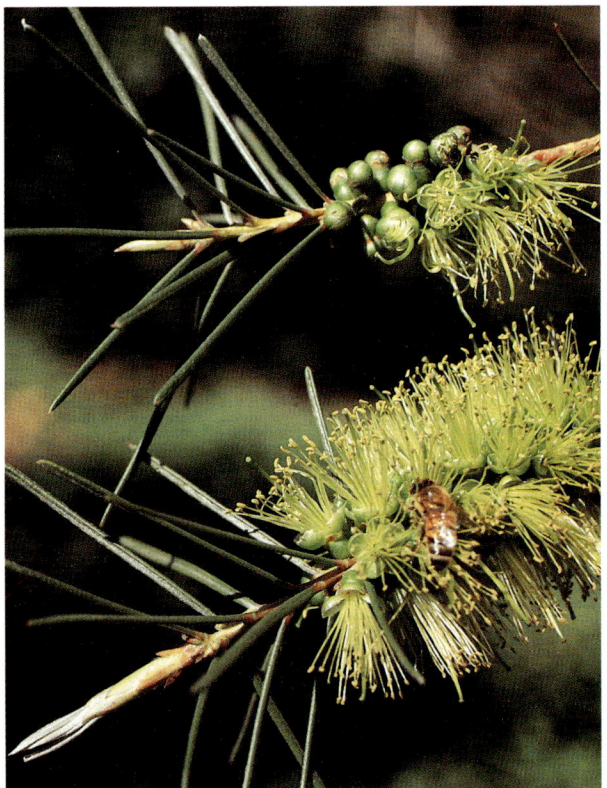

CALLISTEMON viridiflorus
Green Bottlebrush

CALLUNA

Heather,
Ling

☼ C

SPRING–AUTUMN
SLOW/LONG DISPLAY
HT: 50-100cm/1½-3ft/DENSELY SPREADING

Most familiar to inhabitants of northern Europe,
Asia Minor and eastern North America, the genus
Calluna is the famous Scottish Heather of many a
grouse moor and romantic legend. There is only one
species, with innumerable varieties blooming in
shades from white to crimson, and with foliage in
shades of silver, gold or green. All are propagated
vegetatively from 3-5cm tips of one-year-old shoots,
struck in autumn or early spring in cool, moist, leafy
sand. Mature plants prefer a gritty, well-drained,
acid soil with regular water. A cool root run is an
asset, and the plants do well in raised rockeries, or
surrounded by pebbles. Shear faded flowers to keep
bush compact.

CALLUNA *vulgaris*
Scotch Heather

CALOTHAMNUS

Netbush,
One-sided Bottlebrush

☼
T H

SPRING–SUMMER
AVERAGE/LONG DISPLAY
HT: TO 2m/7ft/ERECT OR SPREADING

Untidy in growth, never truly spectacular, the hardy
genus Calothamnus is useful wherever climatic conditions approximate those of its native Western
Australian desert. Highly drought resistant, they
can be relied on in poor or sandy soil, or wherever
wind and salt are a problem. Even light frosts do not
faze them. While growing tips may be destroyed,
flowers are invariably produced on older wood. A
light pruning any time will help keep the bush compact, for it is inclined to grow leggy. Leaves of most
species are needle-like, generally about 4cm long.
The flowers are red, and produced in one-sided clusters, each flower consisting of several bundles of
gold-tipped stamens united at the base. These are
followed by persistent, woody seed capsules. Propagate from seed or cuttings taken in late summer.

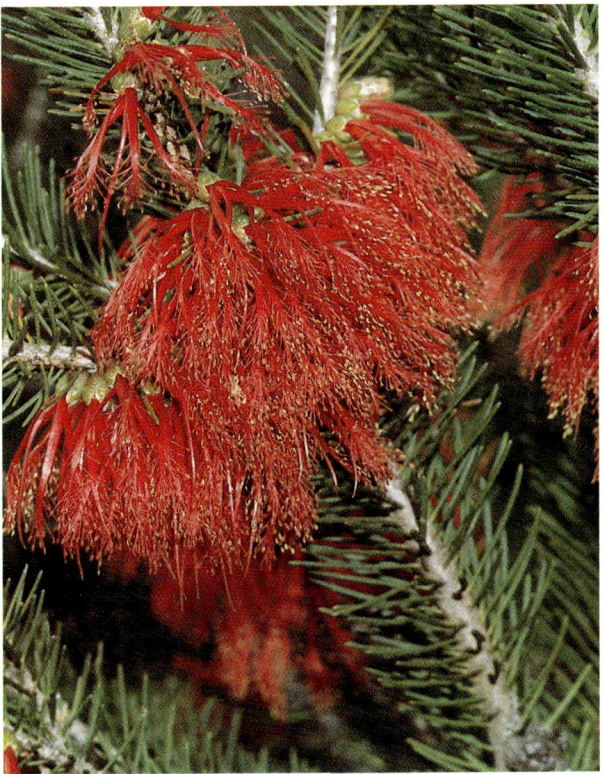

CALOTHAMNUS *villosus*
Silky Netbush

CALOTROPIS FRAGRANT

Giant Milkweed,
Crown Plant,
Bowstring Hemp,
Mudar,
Kapal,
Pua Kalaunu

WARM WEATHER
FAST/POOR DISPLAY
HT: 1.5-4.5m/5-15ft/TALL

Native to Africa and southern Asia, the striking Giant Milkweed, *Calotropis gigantea* has become naturalized in warmer climates world-wide, and is a declared noxious weed in Western Australia. As a shrub, it is rather leggy, its sparse branches clothed with wedge-shaped mealy leaves. But the mauve and pink flowers, which have a charming fragrance, greatly resemble those of the related Stephanotis and are used for lei-making in Hawaii. They may easily be grown from secd, or from cuttings which should be struck under glass and kept dryish. Good drainage is a necessity, and regular heavy pruning after bloom will help promote bushiness and reduce height. *Calotropis* bark yields a strong fibre, the sap makes a type of gutta percha.

CALOTROPIS *gigantea*
Giant Milkweed

CALYCANTHUS FRAGRANT

California Allspice,
Sweet Shrub

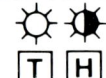

SUMMER
AVERAGE/LONG DISPLAY
HT: 3.5m/12ft

Rather resembling Magnolias, to which they are not related, all 4 species of *Calycanthus* are from North America and share a family classification only with the Asian Chimonanthus. They are deciduous, frost-hardy bushes bearing 20cm glossy leaves that are ovate, pointed and downy on the reverse. The curious flowers, which are quite fragrant, are borne singly on terminal twigs. They look like many-petalled Magnolias, and in the illustrated *C. occidentalis* are 7.5cm in diameter. Like related species, they have purplish-red petals, tinged brown. They may be raised from seed, divisions or, most readily, by layering. Best in full sun.

CALYCANTHUS *occidentalis*
California Allspice

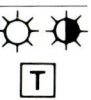

CANTUA buxifolia
Sacred Flower of the Incas

CANTUA

☼ ☀

T

Sacred Flower of the Incas,
Magic Flower

SPRING, OCCASIONALLY OTHER TIMES
AVERAGE/LONG DISPLAY
HT: 1.2m/4-7ft/WEEPING

Whether this gorgeously-blooming shrub really was sacred to the Incas I do not know, but it may well have been, since it comes from the Andes, is scarce in cultivation and very, very beautiful indeed. It enjoys a light, leaf-rich, well-drained soil and a sunny, sheltered position; it is remarkably drought resistant. Propagation is from autumn cuttings struck in sharp sand under glass. *Cantua buxifolia* is said to be reasonably hardy and is grown with wall-shelter in many parts of England. In Australia, I have seen it only in mountain gardens, where the drainage is above suspicion. It develops a rather leggy habit, with slender branches bowed down by the weight of long, tubular flowers. These are purplish-red at their flared tips, with the tubes striped yellow, and borne in dense terminal corymbs. The shrub needs staked support for best display and should be lightly tip-pruned after bloom. Makes a dazzling basket plant when young.

CARISSA FRAGRANT

Natal Plum,
Christ's Thorn

SPRING–SUMMER
FAST/LONG DISPLAY
HT: 1.8-4.5m/6-15ft/UPRIGHT–DENSE

☀ T H

I'd answer queries on how to handle a *Carissa* with the words 'very carefully'. All 20-odd species have wickedly forked spines which can inflict a painful injury. They are very useful plants for a people-proof hedge in warm climates. Warmth is a key to their culture, though smaller-flowered species *C. bispinosa* can be grown elsewhere in an unheated greenhouse. The 5-petalled flowers are fragrant as related Frangipani, and in illustrated *C. grandiflora* are 7.5cm in diameter. They are fairly drought resistant, good seaside plants and need heavy pruning. Propagate from autumn seed (set in the pulpy, scarlet, edible fruit) or from semi-hardwood cuttings struck with heat. Well-drained soil and summer water give the best results.

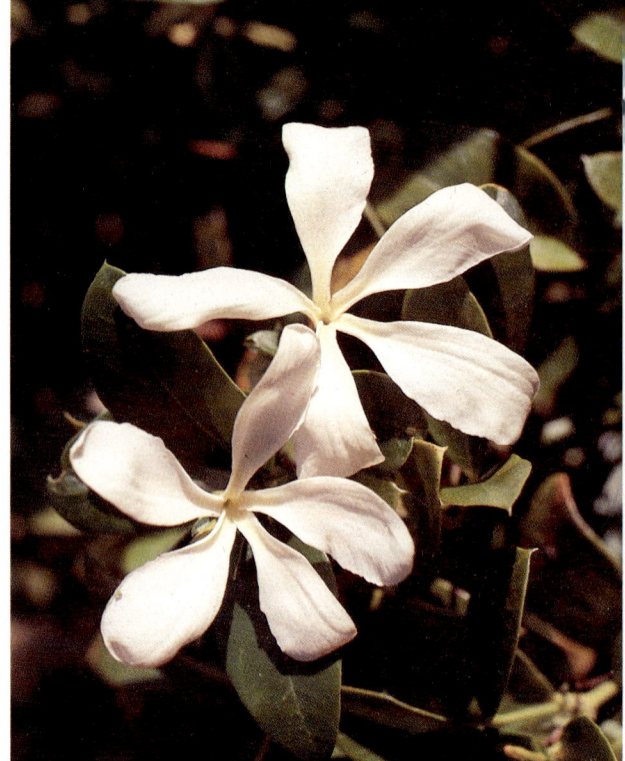

CARISSA grandiflora
Natal Plum

CARPENTERIA FRAGRANT

Tree Anemone

SUMMER
SLOW/SHORT DISPLAY
HT: 2-2.5m/6-8ft/STRAGGLY

☀ ☼ T

Often hard to find because it's difficult to strike from cuttings, lovely Californian *Carpenteria* is best propagated from suckers, or layered in a damp mixture of sand and moss. It will thrive only in full sun (though a semi-shaded position may bring success in hot climates). It hates city pollution, is seen at its best in bright country gardens. *Carpenteria* is evergreen, quite drought resistant and can be killed by over-watering in cold weather. You'll grow it best if you can provide a rich, well-drained soil and prune regularly after bloom to counteract its rather untidy habit. The dark leaves (5-11cm long) are spear-shaped and rather downy. The white, poppy-like flowers are borne singly and are deliciously fragrant.

CARPENTERIA californica
Tree Anemone

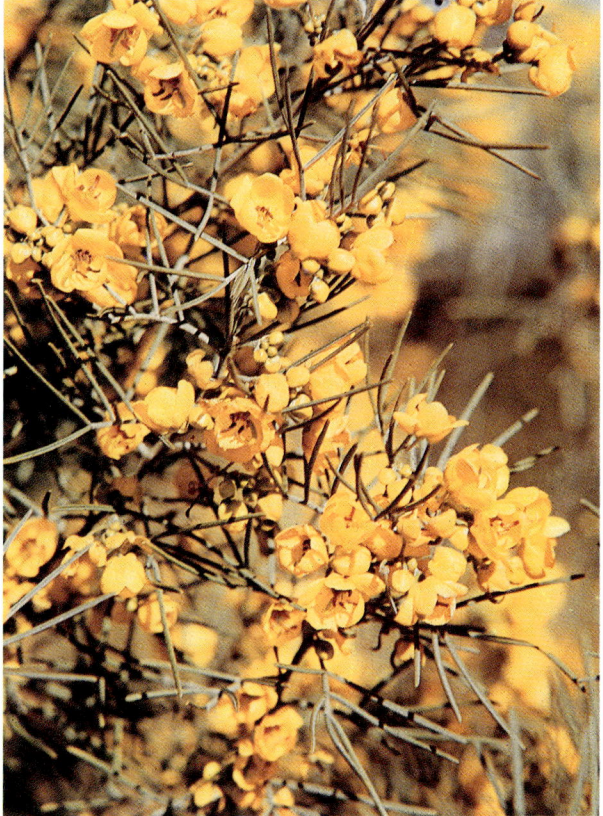

CASSIA corymbosa
Buttercup Bush

CASSIA

Senna Bush,
Buttercup Bush

SPRING–SUMMER
FAST/LONG DISPLAY
HT: 1.5-3m/5-10ft

☼

The very large *Cassia* genus includes some 400 species ranging from annuals to very large trees, and is represented in most warm climates. There is a wide variety of shrubby species for the home garden, mostly easy to raise from seed or from semi-hardened cuttings struck with winter heat. All have pinnate compound leaves. Of the two illustrated species, *C. artemisioides*, the Australian Silver Cassia or Old Man Senna Bush, is a dry climate plant, hardy down to −5°C/23°F. It likes a coarse, well-drained soil and a light but uniform level of moisture. Argentinian *C. corymbosa*, the Buttercup Bush has naturalized all over the world, needs more moisture and self-sows readily. In cooler areas, it should be cut back to 45cm from the ground in late autumn.

CASSIA artemisioides
Old Man Senna Bush

CEANOTHUS X *edwardsii*
California Lilac

CEANOTHUS

California Lilac,
Red Root,
Wild Lilac

SPRING
FAST/LONG DISPLAY
HT: 1.5-2.7m/5-9ft/SPREADING

☼
C T

Though originating in the western United States and Mexico, the lovely California Lilacs (*Ceanothus* spp.) seem to do best in slightly cooler areas. In particular, they enjoy a chilly winter, and do very well in many parts of England. In Australia, they do best in Victoria, Tasmania and mountain districts elsewhere. They are of course not lilacs at all. Certainly they do not share the lovely fragrance, so their popular epithet may be due to the similarity in flower colour. In fact, *Ceanothus* bloom in a wider spectrum than lilacs. Every imaginable shade of blue, violet, mauve, pink and purple can be found among the 40-odd species, and there are whites and greyish tones as well. Some species are deciduous, some evergreen, but the latter are most popular, producing small, alternate leaves of roughly oval shape. These are glossy, finely toothed and deeply veined. The tiny flowers (often as small as 3mm in diameter) develop in showy terminal umbels or panicles. Grow *Ceanothus* in light, gravelly, fast draining soil in full sun. Tip-prune regularly in early years to force a dense habit, then prune away dead flower masses annually. Named hybrids such as illustrated *C.* X *edwardsii* are propagated from semi-hardwood cuttings in spring or autumn. Bottom heat is helpful. *Ceanothus* looks best against a background of dense greenery, and prefers dry summers to humid ones. Species vary from sprawling ground covers to tall tree-like plants.

CESTRUM
(syn HABROTHAMNUS)   SOME FRAGRANT

Cestrum,
Night Jessamine

☼ ☼
T H

SPRING–AUTUMN
FAST/LONG SEASON
HT: 2m/7ft/ERECT–ARCHING CANES

Easy to strike from cuttings, any of the 200 species of
Cestrum makes a good show—and with careful selection, you can have one or another in flower all the
time, either in the open garden or in large tubs. *Ces-
trums* grow fast in any moderately rich, well drained
soil, but need lashings of water and regular doses of
complete fertilizer all through the warm weather.
Regular winter pruning will help strengthen the
trunks and force plenty of new growth. Evergreen,
they are hardy down to 1°C/30°F, and are best
planted against a south-facing wall in England and
North America. *C. nocturnum* is noted for its rich
nocturnal perfume in warmer climates. All parts of
all species are poisonous.

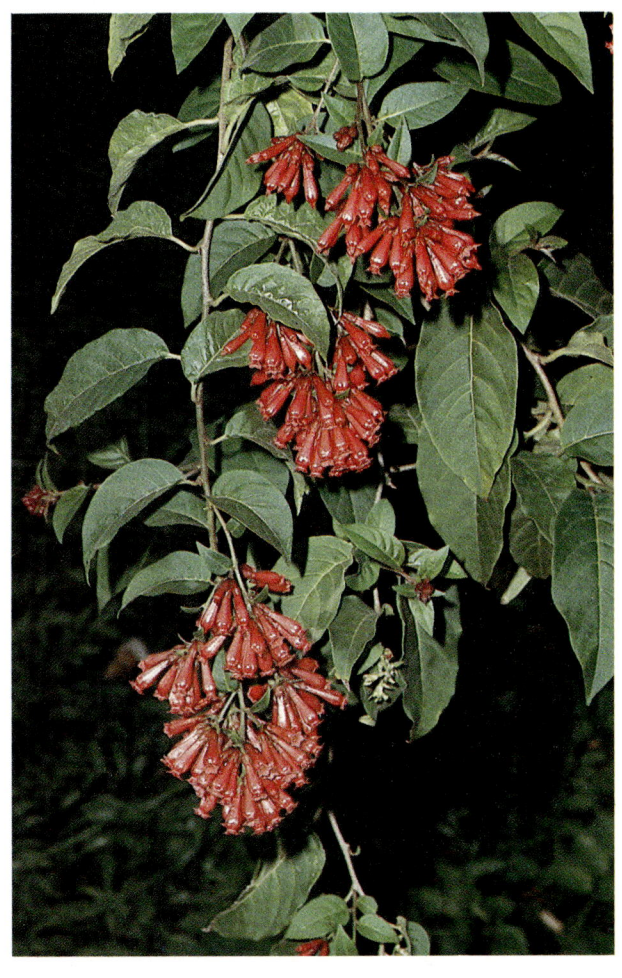

CESTRUM X *newellii*
Red Cestrum

CESTRUM nocturnum
Night Jessamine

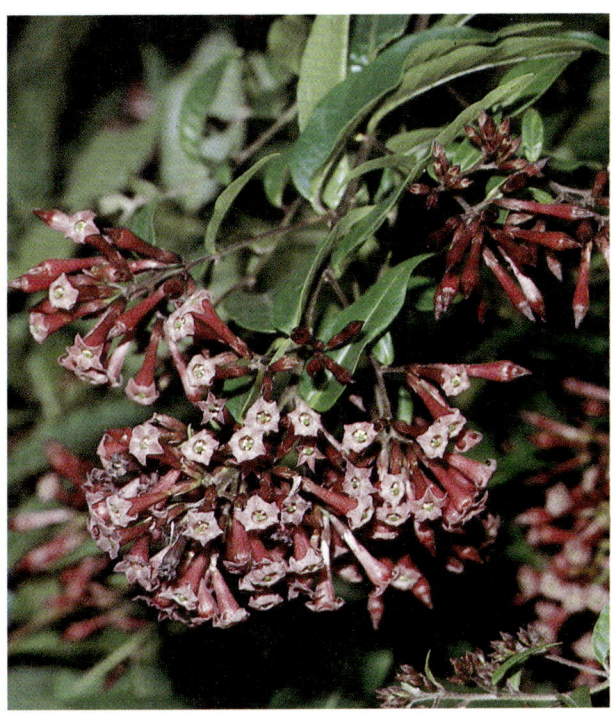

CESTRUM purpureum
Purple Cestrum

CHAENOMELES

Flowering Quince,
Japonica,
Japanese Quince

WINTER–SPRING
AVERAGE/LONG DISPLAY
HT: 60-180cm/2-6ft/SUCKERING

Invaluable for flower arrangers, particularly in cold climates, the Japonicas commence blooming in midwinter and continue for months. Bare, budded stems will open in water indoors. Four species only are known, but many cultivars have been raised, blooming in shades and combinations of white, pink, red and orange. *Chaenomeles* are raised easily from leafy, semi-hardwood cuttings taken in summer or autumn, or by division of the suckering stems. They romp ahead in any well-drained soil, provided the position is in full sun, and should be kept moist throughout summer. All species are hardy down to at least −10°C/14°F. Continued bloom is ensured by pruning out 30% of the older wood each year. The deciduous leaves are shiny and slightly toothed, the blooms typical of the rose family to which they belong, and normally single, though semi-double types are also available. Stems are spiny, and the hard autumn fruit makes a delicious, tangy jelly.

CHAENOMELES *lagenaria* 'Nivalis'
White Flowering Quince

CHAENOMELES X *superba*
'Crimson and Gold' Japonica

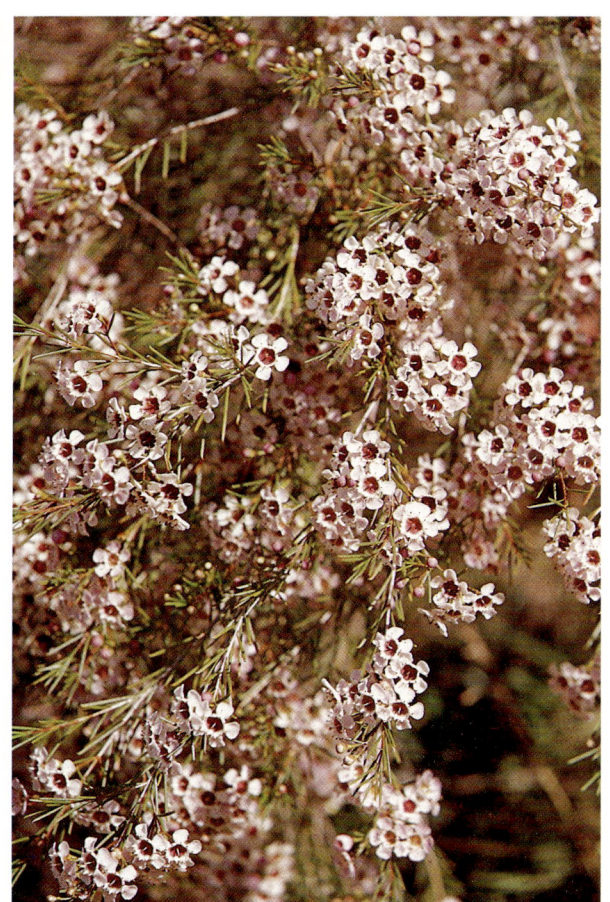

CHAMAELAUCIUM

Wax Flower,
Wax Plant

WINTER–SPRING
FAST/LONG DISPLAY
HT: 80-300cm/2½-10ft/UPRIGHT–ROUNDED

West Australia's *Chamaelauciums* or Wax Plants are widely grown down under, but deserve world-wide popularity in spite of a 'hard-to-grow' reputation which is quite undeserved. It is simply that they prefer a gravelly soil of a rather alkaline balance. Acid soil and too much water are sure to cause premature death, and they do have very brittle roots, so must be planted with extreme care. All species should be propagated from cuttings (grown with warmth and humidity), preferably in late summer. *Chamaelauciums* are members of the myrtle family, have tiny, aromatic leaves and bear their honey-rich 5-petalled, single blooms in small clusters. A light tip-prune after bloom each year will help improve flower yield.

CHAMAELAUCIUM uncinatum
Geraldton Wax

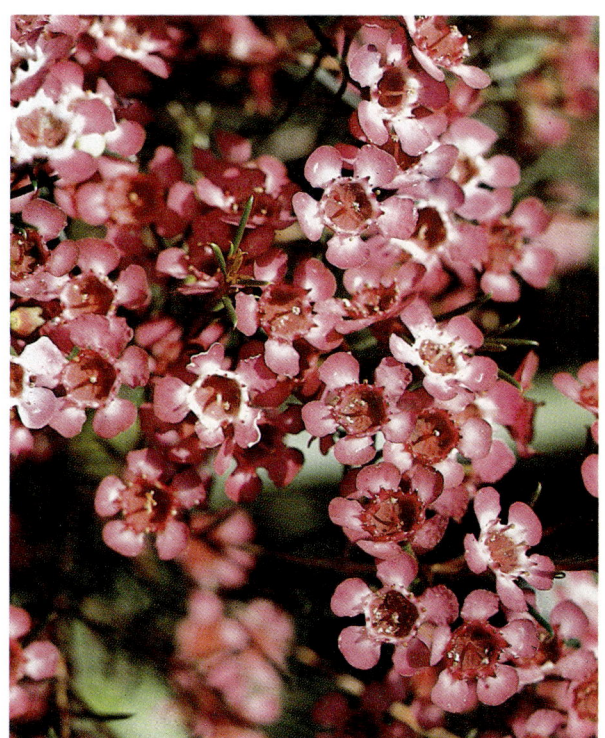

CHAMAELAUCHIUM X 'Purple Splendor'
Purple Wax Plant

CHAMAELAUCIUM megalopetalum
White Waxflower

CHOISYA ternata
Mexican Orange Blossom

CHOISYA FRAGRANT

Mexican Orange Blossom

SPRING
FAST/LONG DISPLAY
HT: 150-180cm/5-6ft/ROUNDED AND DENSE

There is only one species of this elegant evergreen shrub, and yes, it is closely related to the Citrus whose perfume it shares. A great favourite in temperate climate gardens, it needs a certain amount of attention to bloom satisfactorily. Acid soil, rich in humus, is a good starting point, and the shrub's root junction should be set above the surrounding soil level. *Choisya ternata* is propagated from cuttings of firm tips taken in the autumn for striking in a peat-sand mixture. They should be kept warm and humid. A regular pruning keeps the bush dense and produces more bloom. The thin, leathery leaves are aromatic, each consisting of 3 rounded, glossy leaflets. The sweetly fragrant flowers appear in dense axillary clusters and attract bees from everywhere. *Choisya* is hardy down to −9°C/15°F.

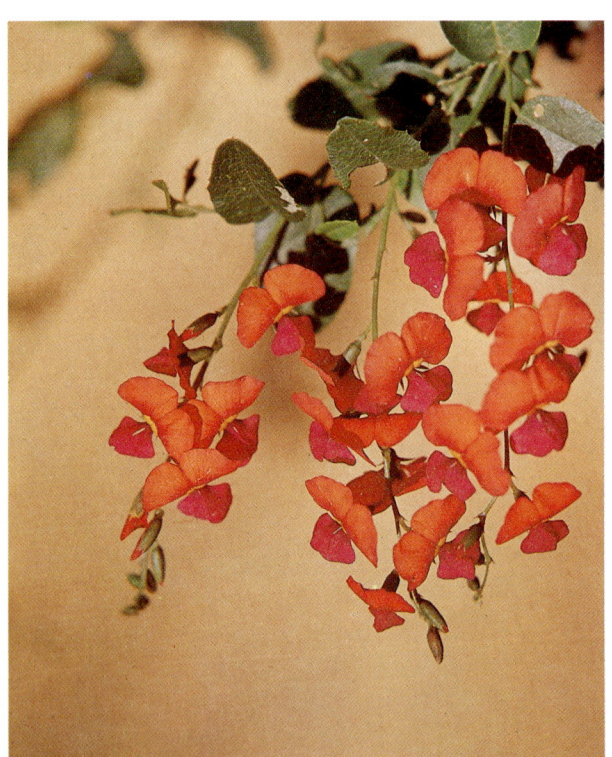

CHORIZEMA cordatum
Heart-leaf Flame Pea

CHORIZEMA

Flame Pea,
Flowering Oak

SPRING
FAST/LONG DISPLAY
HT: TO 1m/3ft

The gaudiest pea-flowers imaginable have brought wide popularity to this small genus of evergreen Australian shrubs. They enjoy a sandy loam, regular water, and need regular heavy pruning to keep them from becoming to untidy. In large native gardens, though, they can be most attractive as sprawling ground cover or in rock-pockets. *Chorizemas* are hardy down to −4°C/24°F, and grow best in full sun, though it must be confessed the colours are brighter in semi-shade. Like most pea-relatives, they can be grown from seed, which should be scarified or soaked for 24 hours in warm water. Alternatively, firm tip-cuttings will strike any time from late summer to midwinter, provided they are kept warm and humid. The glossy 4cm leaves are toothed and somewhat oak-like.

CHRYSOCOMA

Goldilocks

☼ T

SPRING
AVERAGE/LONG DISPLAY
HT: to 60cm/2ft/COMPACT

Closely related to the perennial asters, (Michaelmas and Easter daisies) this dainty South African evergreen can put on an almost blinding display in the rock or paved garden. It enjoys well-drained soil that is almost gravelly—a generous addition of coarse sand and peat will bring your ordinary soil into line. Water with a light hand, but increase the amount as the weather warms up and add a little liquid manure at monthly intervals in spring to force the maximum display of golden pompon flowers. Shear the dwarf bush all over after bloom to keep it compact. Cuttings of half-ripened shoots are easy to strike under glass in late summer. *Chrysocoma coma-aurea* is the only species.

CHRYSOCOMA coma-aurea
Goldilocks

CISTUS

Rock Rose

☼ T

SPRING–SUMMER
FAST/LONG DISPLAY
HT: 30-180cm/1-6ft/SPREADING

Wonderful evergreen shrubs from sun-baked shores of the Mediterranean, the 20-odd species of *Cistus* are the perfect choice for poor or sandy soil, for exposed banks or seaside cliffs. Most of them remain compact, particularly when pinched back regularly. They are remarkably drought resistant, need little water once established—but as a corollary do not like humidity. Propagate from spring-sown seed, but young plants should be pricked out as soon as possible, for they don't like later disturbance. Firm tip-cuttings can be taken in autumn, struck in a cool greenhouse. This is a good safety precaution anyway, for the plants can be destroyed by temperatures below −9°C/15°F. Flower colours are white, rose, lilac, purple, red, with the petals often basally blotched in black, crimson or yellow. Leaves are often silvery and sage-like.

CISTUS X 'Silver Pink'
Sage-leaf Rock Rose

CLERODENDRUM

SOME FRAGRANT

Glory Bower,
Butterfly Bush,
Pagoda Flower

☼ ☀
T H

SPRING–AUTUMN
AVERAGE/LONG DISPLAY
HT: 60-300cm/2-10ft

Most variable in their habits and appearance, 300 species of *Clerodendrum* grow wild in parts of Africa and South-east Asia. Often shrubby, there are also climbing and tree-like species among them. They are great favourites in warm climate gardens. Most can be grown from ripe seed, but are more usually propagated from semi-hardwood cuttings taken in autumn. They do well in a rich, leafy soil, need year-round water, more generous in summer. *C. fragrans* (often called Cashmere Bouquet) is a broad-leafed shrub bearing compact corymbs of fragrant, double pink and white flowers. *C. paniculatum* bears pagoda-like terminal spikes of scarlet bloom. Taller-growing *C. ugandense* displays panicles of butterfly-shaped bloom in two shades of blue, needs heavy pruning.

CLERODENDRUM fragrans
Cashmere Bouquet

CLERODENDRUM paniculatum
Pagoda Flower

CLERODENDRUM ugandense
Blue Butterfly Bush

COLEONEMA AROMATIC

Diosma,
Breath of Heaven,
Confetti Bush

WINTER–SPRING
AVERAGE/LONG DISPLAY
HT: 1.5m/5ft/BUN-SHAPED

Neat, evergreen shrubs from South Africa, *Coleonemas* have aromatic, heath-like foliage, though belonging to the Citrus family. They grow best in a rich but well-drained soil, are favourites for planting on banks or in groups as lawn specimens. With continuous light pruning, they can be trained as light, informal hedges, though flower loss will result. Winter moisture stimulates bloom, but mature plants will endure drought along the coast. *Coleonemas* are easily propagated from soft tip cuttings taken in late summer. These should be struck in a sharp sand/peat mixture with bottom heat and misting. The tiny 5-petalled flowers appear in many shades of pink. There is a white flowered species, and one with golden foliage.

COLEONEMA album
Breath of Heaven

COLEONEMA pulchrum
Confetti Bush, Diosma

CONVOLVULUS

Bush Morning Glory,
Silver Bush

☼ T

SPRING–SUMMER
FAST/LONG DISPLAY
HT: 60-120cm/2-4ft/COMPACT

Think of *Convolvulus* and you normally visualize the pink or blue flowered Morning Glory vines twining round cottage doors. But south-European *C. cneorum* is definitely a shrub, and a compact, bushy one at that. It may be propagated from seed, but is easier to grow from heeled cuttings of basal shoots taken in summer for striking in a damp mixture of peat and sand. The Silver Bush likes to sunbake in a light, sandy soil where it will develop into a compact, densely-foliaged plant in no time at all. The pointed, lance-shaped leaves have a satiny texture and are covered with silver-silky hairs on both sides. The white 2.5cm trumpet flowers are flushed with pale pink, appear in dense terminal clusters.

CONVOLVULUS *cneorum*
Bush Morning Glory

COROKIA FRAGRANT

Wire-netting Bush

☼ T

SPRING–SUMMER
AVERAGE/LONG DISPLAY
HT: TO 3m/10ft/SPARSE,
    SPREADING GROWTH

Hardy down to −5°C/23°F, New Zealand's dainty Wire-netting Bush makes an interesting informal ground cover, but is probably more effective when pruned regularly to force denser growth. In this guise it can make an effective hedge, or a useful addition to the sheltered seaside garden. Flowering best in full sun, it appreciates a moderately rich soil and light water year round. Propagate from seed or firm 8cm tip-cuttings taken in autumn. *Corokia cotoneaster* grows every which way but where you wanted, zigging and zagging in all direction, producing tiny roundish leaves and, in season, a veritable cloud of bright yellow, star-shaped blooms at the leaf axils. These may be borne singly or in small clusters, are lightly fragrant.

COROKIA *cotoneaster*
Wire-netting Bush

CORONILLA

Crown Vetch

SPRING–SUMMER
FAST/SHORT DISPLAY
HT: 120cm/4ft

Among the most brilliantly flowering genera in the pea family, 20-odd *Coronilla* species bloom (as Henry Ford might have said) in any colour you like so long as it's yellow! Their name is a very old one, meaning 'little crowns'. The Crown Vetch, *C. glauca*, is most commonly seen, a dense, 1m evergreen bush, always with an odd number of leaflets on either side of each leaf. The yellow pea blossoms appear everywhere and are quite fragrant in the daylight hours. Grow *Coronillas* from seed, cuttings, layers or divisions—they are remarkably easy to propagate. All species are native to areas around the Mediterranean, and prefer similar climatic conditions with an open, well-drained soil.

CORONILLA glauca
Crown Vetch

COTINUS

Smokebush,
Venetian Sumach

SPRING–SUMMER
AVERAGE/LONG DISPLAY
HT: 3-4m/10-13ft

While the Smokebush does bloom (and quite heavily at that), its principal display is a mass of tiny flower *stems* which become covered with spidery hairs after blossom-fall. These stem clusters persist for months, taking on the appearance of puffs of low-lying red smoke. *Cotinus coggyria* is a tall-growing bush, and completely deciduous, turning on quite a dazzling display of autumn colour in cooler areas. It should be pruned heavily in late winter to reduce the number of growth buds on each shoot by two-thirds. Grow it in well drained soil with light but regular watering. *Cotinus* may be propagated from spring seed, root cuttings, layers or hardwood stem cuttings taken in winter. These cuttings should be dusted with hormone rooting powder before attempting to strike in sharp sand.

COTINUS coggyria
Smokebush

CROTALARIA *agatiflora*
Canary-bird Bush

CROTALARIA

Canary-bird Bush,
Rattle-box

☼

ALL YEAR, PERIODICALLY
FAST/LONG DISPLAY
HT: 2-4m/4-13ft

T H

Gardeners in cool northern hemisphere areas may well be unaware of the very large *Crotalaria* genus. Its 500-odd species are great favourites in warmer climates, but are just not frost hardy. Both illustrated species do well in any temperate to tropical climate in a moderately rich, well-drained soil. Both should be pruned after bloom to help keep them in bounds and induce a second flush of bloom. *Crotalarias* can be grown from seed which should first be soaked for at least 12 hours, or from soft tip-cuttings taken for striking in spring. *C. agatiflora* (syn *C. laburnifolia*) has soft green leaves consisting of three leaflets, just like the European Laburnum. Before opening, its yellow-green flowers look exactly like birds suspended by their beaks. *C. semperflorens* has simple, heavily-ribbed ovate leaves with golden pea-flowers in a terminal spike. The ripe, puffy seed pods of both species have given rise to the name Rattle-box.

CROTALARIA *semperflorens*
Indian Rattle-box

CYTISUS

Broom

SPRING–SUMMER
FAST/LONG DISPLAY
HT: 1-4.5m/3-15ft/MOSTLY WEEPING

☼
C T

What *Crotalarias* are to the warm climate, so *Cytisus* is to cool temperate areas. A smaller genus, with all 50 species native to the Mediterranean and Atlantic islands, *Cytisus* bears the same showy pea-flowers, though borne in greater profusion over a longer period. The colour range is also wider, including shades of pink, white, cream, tan and mahogany red as well as basic yellow. Of the illustrated species, C. *praecox* and C. *scoparius* are propagated from ripe shoots, taken in autumn; C. *battandieri* (a much larger plant) grows better from seed. All enjoy a poor quality, slightly acid soil, and need regular water throughout spring and summer. The Scotch Broom is evergreen, the others deciduous, with a generally weeping habit. All have silky leaves of three leaflets, and a strong smell, not necessarily pleasant.

CYTISUS *praecox*
Warminster Broom

CYTISUS *scoparius*
Scotch Broom

CYTISUS *battandieri*
Atlas Broom

DAPHNE odora rubra
Sweet Daphne

DAPHNE X burkwoodii
Hybrid Daphne

DAPHNE FRAGRANT

Daphne,
Garland Flower

WINTER–SPRING
AVERAGE/LONG DISPLAY
HT: 30-180cm/1-6ft

☼ ☀
C T

Once upon a time, in far off Arcadia, there lived a sprightly wood nymph, Daphne. One day, while lazing in the sun, she caught the roving eye of Apollo, the sun god. In a flash, he was there beside her, and Daphne, fearing the worst, began frantically praying to her favourite goddesses for help. And help they did! Daphne's arms turned to sleek branches with shining leaves, her feet took root, and she became one of the prettiest flowering shrubs ever seen. And that's why you'll always find *Daphne* blooming in shady places, as a warning to other nymphs to stay out of the sun. *That,* according to the ancient Greeks, was the origin of the charming, European *Daphne laureola,* a species not much grown since the discovery of its more beautiful cousins in Asia. We now know there are some 35 species of these delight-fully fragrant winter and spring flowering shrubs, scattered in the wild everywhere from Spain to Japan. They are favourites in all gardens short of the subtropics. Most are of hillside, woodland origin and moderately hardy in temperatures down to −8°C/ 21°F. They like a well-drained, slightly acid soil, though *D. cneorum* will tolerate limey soil, provided there's plenty of leaf mould mixed in. Only light watering is needed, especially in summer, with a meagre ration of complete fertilizer immediately after bloom. Over-watering in summer will lead to a variety of fungus diseases, especially collar rot, which will put paid to an apparently healthy plant in no time. Best place *Daphnes* in a slightly raised position, with the root junction above soil level, and let the surface dry out thoroughly between summer waterings. Pruning is a pleasure: only regular, generous picking of the flowering stems is needed. Most *Daphnes* are evergreen, with shining, spear-shaped leaves. The flowers are 4-petalled, with a curious waxy, sparkling texture. They are borne in terminal clusters. Propagate from leafy tip-cuttings struck in midsummer, under glass. *D. cneorum* will grow from seed.

DAPHNE cneorum
Garland Flower

DAPHNE odora marginata
Winter Daphne

DARWINIA FRAGRANT

Scent Myrtle

SPRING–SUMMER
AVERAGE/LONG DISPLAY
HT: 1m/3ft

Compact, heath-like shrubs included in the myrtle family, Australia's 25-odd species of *Darwinia* are useful shrubs for sandy, acid soil. Easily propagated from lateral cuttings taken in spring or autumn and struck in sharp sand, they like a well-draining position and thrive with a minimum of water and an occasional light dressing of organic fertilizer. The evergreen leaves are small and aromatic, generally sharply pointed and linear, and of a light green colour. The flowers appear in both terminal and axillary clusters and their petals are so inconspicuous they are often mistaken for leaves. The showy part is a cluster of 10 red and white stamens which protrude in a pincusion effect. All species feature this same colour scheme.

DARWINIA fascicularis
Scent Myrtle

DENDROMECON FRAGRANT

Tree Poppy

SPRING–SUMMER
AVERAGE/LONG DISPLAY
HT: 3m/10ft/ROUNDED TO TREE-LIKE

One of California's most beautiful native shrubs, *Dendromecon rigida* is sometimes known as the California Tree Poppy—and that's exactly what it is—a member of the poppy family that has adapted into a hard-wooded perennial form. There is only one species, though with many local varieties including one, *D. rigida harfordii*, which has been recorded to a height of 6m on California's coastal islands. *Dendromecon* likes dry, gravelly soil and a well drained position; may be propagated from seed (which is very slow to germinate) or cuttings of well-ripened summer shoots struck in sharp sand with some heat. The evergreen leaves are simple, leathery, generally pointed and a curious shade of grey-green. Given a warm sheltered spot, it will produce masses of pleasantly fragrant, 7.5cm poppy flowers in warm weather, each a brilliant shade of golden yellow.

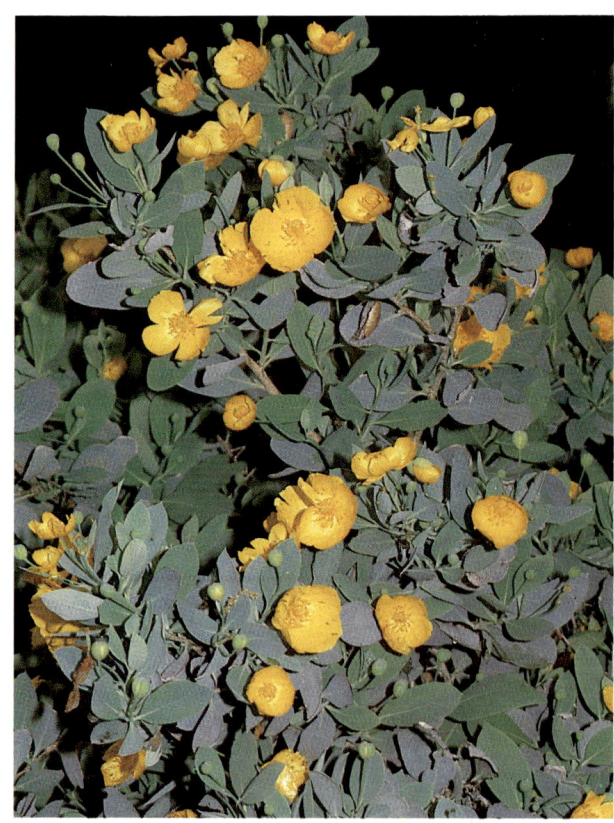

DENDROMECON rigida
Island Tree Poppy

DEUTZIA

Wedding Bells

☼ ☀
C T

SPRING–SUMMER
AVERAGE/LONG DISPLAY
HT: 1.5-2m/5-7ft/ARCHING STEMS

Splendid oriental shrubs that bloom with late spring bulbs and continue to early summer, *Deutzias* are closely related to Philadelphus (which see) but without their rich mock-orange perfume. As compensation they are notable for the grace and delicacy of their long, arching canes, which literally bend under the weight of hanging flower clusters. Most of the 40-odd species need a rich, fast-draining soil, and grow readily from semi-hardwood cuttings taken in summer. Deciduous, *Deutzias* produce long, pointed leaves 8-12cm in length, with terminal panicles of single, starry blooms in white, pink or mauve. After bloom, prune away as many as one-third of older canes completely. Allow plenty of room: frost-hardy *Deutzias* are normally far wider than high.

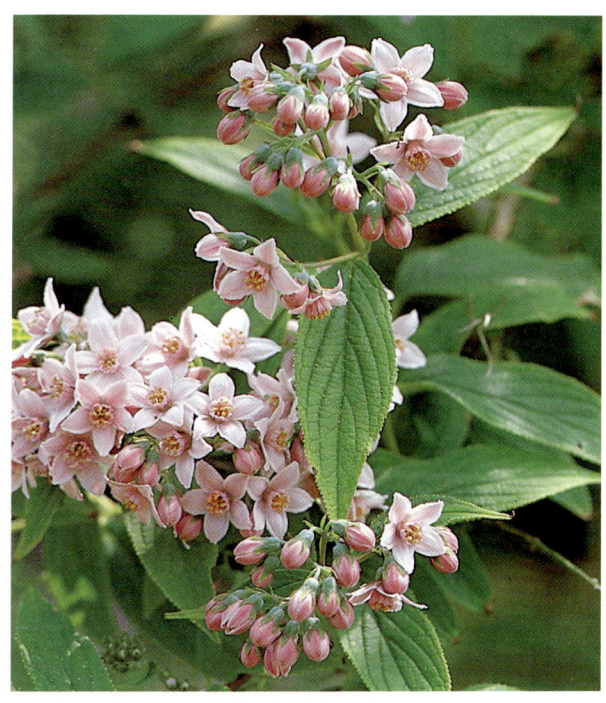

DEUTZIA longifolia
Longleaf Deutzia

DEUTZIA gracilis
Slender Deutzia

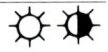

DREJERELLA guttata
Shrimp Plant

DREJERELLA
(syn BELOPERONE)

Shrimp Plant,
Prawn Plant

☼ ☀

T H

SPRING–AUTUMN
FAST/LONG DISPLAY
HT: TO 1m/3ft/SPREADING

Nature was working overtime as a mimic when she designed this flower, for a bush in full bloom really does appear to be festooned with shrimps. The pinkish-brown petal forms are actually bracts, or modified leaves, and the tiny white true flowers are almost hidden among them. *Drejerella* grows most strongly in a rich, well-drained soil, colouring best in semi-shade. But overall it is a weak, sprawling

plant and needs regular light pruning in late winter to remove spindly growth and encourage new flowering shoots from the base. In tropical or subtropical climates it is almost continuously in bloom, but will flower remarkably well in cooler areas, particularly along the coast. Anywhere in fact that temperatures do not drop below 7°C/45°F. In cooler climates it can be raised as a showy container plant or taken under glass during the winter. *Drejerella* can be raised easily from soft tip-cuttings or semi-hardwood cuttings taken in summer or autumn, or from winter prunings provided they can be struck in a warm, humid place. Though *Drejerella* seems to be its current botanical name, it is often listed as *Beloperone*, or as *Justicia brandegeana*. The pinkish variety is most common, but there is also a lime green and yellow type, *D. guttata aurea*.

DRYANDRA

Bush Rose

☼ T

SPRING
AVERAGE/LONG DISPLAY
HT: TO 3m/10ft

Named for a botanical contemporary of Joseph
Banks, the West Australian *Dryandras* include some
of the most spectacular blooms in the Protea family.
Unfortunately, few of the 50 species can be grown
away from their natural conditions of dry heat and
sandy soil, but the smaller flowered *D. polycephala*
has been grown on Australia's east coast and
elsewhere. It must be propagated from seed, and
should be planted in a sheltered spot and left to its
own devices. It cannot abide lime, and does not like
cultivation nearby. The 10cm leaves are thin and
saw-toothed, the golden flower heads borne both
terminally and on laterals. When picked, *Dryandra*
stems last for years, only the foliage fading.

DRYANDRA *polycephala*
Small-flowered Dryandra

EDGWORTHIA FRAGRANT

Paperbush,
Yellow Daphne,
Mitsumata

☼
C T

WINTER–SPRING
AVERAGE/SHORT DISPLAY
HT: 1-1.8m/4-6ft/SPREADING

Closely related to Daphnes, the Paperbush, *Edgwor-thia*, strongly resembles them except in colour, for
the silky grey-green buds open to snowy 4-petalled
blooms lined with rich, egg-yolk yellow. The perfume of their showy terminal flower clusters is
equally rich. *Edgworthia* is deciduous, producing
masses of 8-14cm oval leaves as the flowers fade.
These are crowded mostly towards the end of
branches, which are so flexible they can be knotted
without breaking. *Edgworthia* is frost hardy only in
sheltered positions, must be grown in well-drained
acid soil, for it is a mountain plant like the true
Daphnes. Plenty of summer water is needed, and
propagation is from cuttings struck in sand under
glass, or by layering. The entire plant is tough and
fibrous, was used for papermaking in Japan.

EDGWORTHIA *papyrifera*
Yellow Daphne

EMBOTHRIUM coccineum
Chilean Firebush

EMBOTHRIUM

Chilean Firebush

☼ T

SPRING–SUMMER
AVERAGE/LONG DISPLAY
HT: 5m/15ft/ERECT

This rather large evergreen shrub from Chile is sometimes listed as a small tree but it does not have a true tree's single trunk. It suckers heavily and will in time develop into a dense planting. It demands a loose, peaty soil that is either neutral or acid, and will not tolerate lime or animal manures. Its propagation is not easy, as cuttings do not seem to strike, so you're left with the slower alternative of seed, which should be sown early spring in a standard seed raising mix at a temperature of 13°C/55°F. Prick out into individual pots when large enough, and grow on for two years before finally setting out in spring. Suckers from a large plant can also be severed and grown on. A member of the Protea family, *Embothrium* bears leathery, spear-shaped leaves and produces startling racemes of tubular scarlet flowers, their 4 petals reflexed to display a protruding style. Strictly for the cooler temperate climate, *Embothrium* is remarkably frost hardy.

ENKIANTHUS
(syn MELIDORA)

Chinese Bellflower FRAGRANT

SPRING AND AUTUMN
SLOW/LONG DISPLAY
HT: 1-2m/3-6ft/ERECT

☼ ◐
C T

Grow Azaleas and Ericas—you can grow the dainty bellflower *Enkianthus*, a slow-moving lover of semi-shaded places where the acid to neutral soil is rich in leaf mould and always well drained. A background of evergreen shrubbery helps disguise the rather spidery habit and accent the pale flowers and vivid autumn colour. *Enkianthus* species are hardy down to −8°C/17°F, and do best in country gardens, for they resent air pollution. In ideal conditions, they produce masses of sharply pointed leaves as the flowers fade. These last until cooler weather turns them into a riot of autumn colour. The lightly fragrant bellflowers, like lilies of the valley, are borne in terminal umbels, each flower hanging from a slender stem. Propagate *Enkianthus* from seed, or from autumn cuttings of lateral shoots taken with a heel. Dip in hormone powder and strike in a standard sand/peat mix under glass. Flowers may be white, pink, red or green.

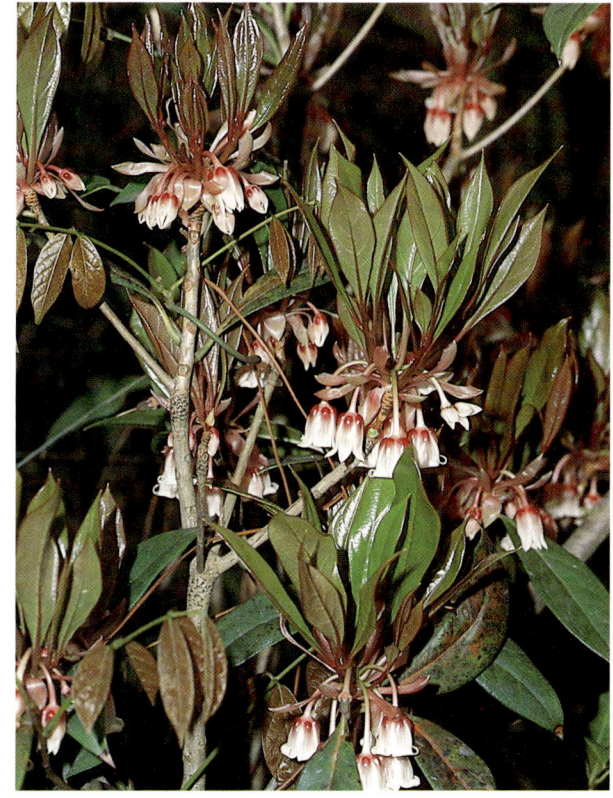

ENKIANTHUS quinqueflorus
Chinese Bellflower

ENKIANTHUS perulatus
Japanese Bellflower

ERANTHEMUM

Blue Sage,
Limeng-sugat,
Guerit Petit

☼ ◑
T H

WINTER–SPRING
FAST/LONG DISPLAY
HT: 60-100cm/2-4ft/BUSHY

This charming shrub from South-east Asia is easy to grow anywhere the minimum day temperature stays above 13°C/55°F. It has handsome heavily-veined leaves and pushes ahead from spring cuttings rooted in a glass of water! For maximum display, plant several cuttings as a clump in leaf-rich, well drained soil with a dressing of milled animal manure. Fertilize every three months, keep up the water in warm weather, tapering off until flowering is over, after which you can prune the plants heavily, resting them until late spring. The purple-eyed blue flowers appear in long, terminal spikes from among pale green bracts. *Eranthemum* also makes a good container plant.

ERANTHEMUM *pulchellum*
Blue Sage

EREMOPHILA

Emu Bush,
Poverty Bush

☼
T H

ALL YEAR
SLOW/SPARSE DISPLAY
HT: TO 1.5m/5ft

Found exclusively in Australia, many of the 60-odd species of *Eremophila* have been exported to other drought-prone areas, producing an invaluable display where almost nothing else will grow. They are quite drought resistant; adore hot, dry climates; and reward a minimum of care with a welcome sprinkling of flower colour at any time of the year. They come in all sizes, with flowers in many different colours, but the most attractive and typical species are spreading bushes with grey-green, lightly haired foliage and tubular heath-type flowers of vivid scarlet. These appear at leaf-axils all over the plant. *Eremophilas* grow easily from cuttings taken with a heel in autumn and struck in a sharp, sandy mix. Grow them on for a year or two in a slightly alkaline compost before planting out. Water sparsely.

EREMOPHILA *glabra*
Emu Bush

ERICA

Heath,
Heather

SPECIES FOR EVERY SEASON
SLOW/LONG DISPLAY
HT: 20-450cm/8-180in/VARIABLE

☼
C T

One of the most variable shrub genera, the *Ericas* include some 500 species, all but thirty of them from South Africa. They are beautiful, extraordinarily floriferous plants with some species in bloom at any time of the year. They are also, with rare exceptions, extraordinarily fussy plants with a very pronounced group of likes and dislikes. For this reason, in European gardens, they are generally grown on their own in raised beds sited in full sun. The beds are raised because *Ericas* must have the perfect drainage of their native mountainsides. The ideal growing medium consists of two parts fibrous peat and one part silver sand. They cannot abide lime or any type of animal manure, and are best watered with pure, unpolluted water. They need constant moisture, and a year-round mulch of pebbles or other lime-free

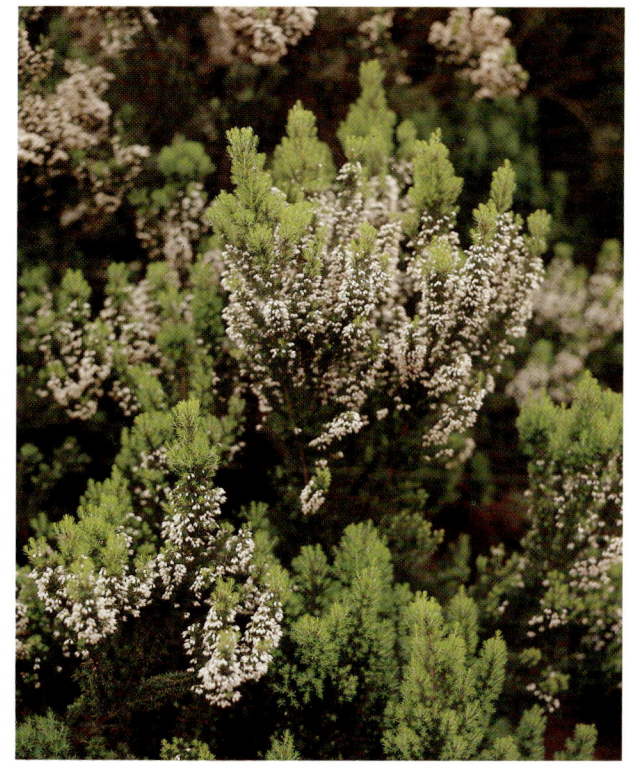

ERICA arborea alpina
Alpine Tree Heath

ERICA cinerea
Bell Heather

material. Most species can be raised easily if slowly from seed—though plants are unlikely to come true if you grow more than one species. The practical gardener will propagate them from 2cm tip-cuttings taken in autumn or early winter and struck in a constantly moist sand/peat mix. The illustrated species vary widely in both height and habit from *E. cinerea* (a 20cm mat-forming shrub) to *E. arborea* (a 450cm tree-like plant). All have small, evergreen linear or needle leaves and flowers that are either tubular or bell-shaped. These are slightly fragrant in the mass, and much appreciated by bees. All species can be lightly shaped by pruning away flowered shoots—but *only* of the past year's growth.

ERICA X 'Aurora'
Hybrid Cape Heath

ERICA vagans 'Lyonesse'
White Cornish Heath

ERIOCEPHALUS FRAGRANT

Woolflower

☼ T

WINTER–SPRING
AVERAGE/LONG DISPLAY
HT: 50-100cm/18-40in/SPREADING

South Africa's *Eriocephalus* species are members of the daisy family, though they don't look much like it. The commonly seen species *E. africanus* or Woolflower is a dwarf, spreading shrub that likes sandy acid soil, full sun and will even stand a certain amount of frost in a sheltered position. Useful at the seaside, it is also drought tolerant. Grow it from cuttings of young shoots and give room to spread. Its needle-like leaves are silky, the late winter flowers white with gold or purple centres, and borne in dense terminal umbels. They are quite fragrant, and after bloom, the seed heads expand into woolly balls that are sometimes dried for decoration. Prune occasionally to restore shape.

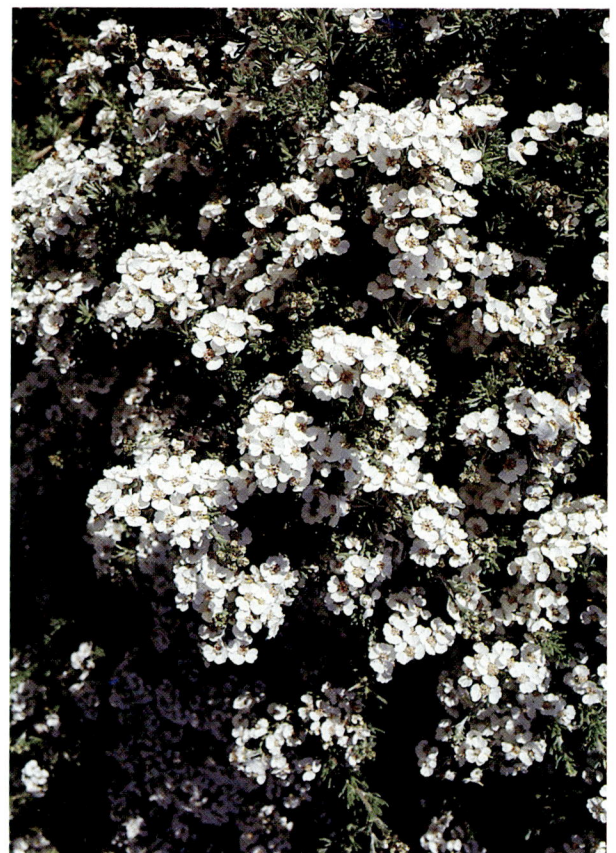

ERIOCEPHALUS africanus
Woolflower

ERIOSTEMON FRAGRANT

Waxflower,
Native Daphne

☼ ◑

 T

WINTER–SPRING
AVERAGE/LONG DISPLAY
HT: 1m-4ft/ROUNDED

Gardeners in many temperate climates are in friendly competition growing Australia's delightful native Waxflowers. There are 30-odd species with one from nearby New Caledonia. The favourite by far is *Eriostemon myoporoides* which does, at a distance resemble the Asiatic Daphnes. The leaves however are narrower, and the flowers not as fragrant as in the true Daphnes, though they have a sharp, citrus perfume. *E. myoporoides* can be grown from seed, which should be soaked in warm water for 24 hours before early spring sowing, or from semi-hardened cuttings taken in autumn. *Eriostemons* are susceptible to root-rot, should be set in a fast-draining compost of leaf-mould and silver sand. Some gardeners help both growth and lifespan by grafting onto shoots of *Correa alba*.

ERIOSTEMON myoporoides
Long-leaf Waxflower

ESCALLONIA FRAGRANT

(no popular name)

☼ ◐
T

SUMMER–AUTUMN
FAST/LONG DISPLAY
HT: 4.5m/15ft/TREE-LIKE

All but one of 60 natural *Escallonia* species are ever-green. They come from Chile, but have been exten-sively hybridized in both California and England. Sturdy, glossy-leafed shrubs, they are not really frost-hardy, enjoying a well-drained but compost-rich soil and plenty of moisture in summer. They are best propagated from 10cm cuttings of half-ripe, non-flowered shoots taken with a heel in late summer. Strike them under glass. A light pruning to remove spent flower heads only is advisable, though they can be pruned more heavily if you risk the sacrifice of many flowers. These vary from white to red, are lightly fragrant and borne in terminal, hang-ing clusters.

ESCALLONIA 'Crimson Spire'
Hybrid Escallonia

EUPATORIUM

(syn HEBECLINIUM)

Mist Flower,
Thoroughwort,
Boneset,
Shrub Ageratum

☼ ◐
T H

SPRING
FAST/LONG DISPLAY
HT: 2m/7ft/LEAFY

An enormous genus of shrubs and herbs, mostly from the Americas, *Eupatoriums* are frequently mis-taken for overgrown Ageratums, which they strongly resemble. Mauve-flowered species make a splendid contrast to pink spring blossom, and are often planted in a mixed border. They need a winter temperature of at least 10°C/50°F to look at all happy, so are probably not familiar to many north-ern hemisphere gardeners. In the right climate, they are easily propagated from twiggy, semi-hardwood cuttings with short internodes, struck under glass in autumn. Grow them in an enriched, well-drained soil with plenty of water to develop the large (up to 20cm) furry leaves and massive panicles of mauve or violet puffball flowers. After blooming, prune flowered stems lightly to avoid having clouds of seed blowing all over the garden.

EUPATORIUM magalophyllum
Mist Flower

EUPHORBIA

Poinsettia,
Crown of Thorns,
Flor de Nino

WINTER–SUMMER ☼ ☀
FAST/LONG DISPLAY T H
HT: 45-300cm/1½-10ft/ROUNDED CROWN

Familiar enough to houseplant fans everywhere, the
shrubby species of *Euphorbia* are probably the best
known members of the genus, which also includes
more than 1000 annuals, perennials and succu-
lents—many with little resemblance to the illustrated species. What do they have in common?
First, an unpleasant, milky sap, usually poisonous.
Secondly, spectacular flower-like arrangements
which are not flowers at all, but a series of highly
coloured bracts or modified leaves.

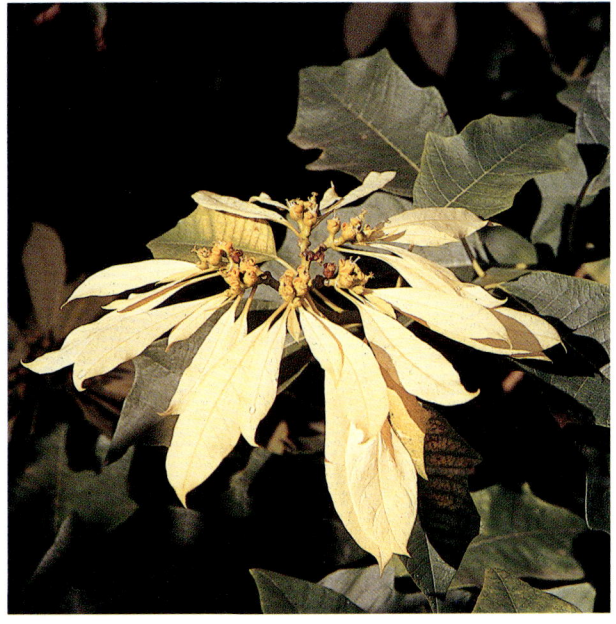

EUPHORBIA pulcherrima alba
White Poinsettia

EUPHORBIA 'Henrietta Ecke'
Double Poinsettia

Of the shrub species, the hollow-stemmed Poinsettia, *E. pulcherrima*, is the showiest, its dazzling display stimulated by the shortening days of winter. It likes well-drained soil, plenty of water and is normally grown from divisions, or from soft tip cuttings taken in summer and autumn. These are potted up individually in sharp sand and kept warm and humid until growth is seen. Prune heavily after bloom, shortening flowered stems by at least half.

The Crown of Thorns, *E. milii*, is a spiny, succulent plant, deciduous in cooler areas. It is easily propagated from spring cuttings, dried off before striking in sharp sand. Fairly drought resistant and hardy down to 7°C/45°F, it likes light, regular water in summer, tapering off in its winter resting period. The scarlet bracts appear in spring with the foliage, and intermittent blooms are borne throughout the warm months. Pruning is needed only to control size. It prefers a slightly acid, well-drained soil.

E. leucocephala, the Flor de Nino (Flower of the Christ-child), is from Central America, and propagated in the same way as the Poinsettia. It can additionally be grown from seed and its bracts are always white.

EUPHORBIA leucocephala
Flor de Nino, Pascuita

EUPHORBIA milii
Crown of Thorns

EURYOPS

Yellow Marguerite,
Brighteyes

WINTER–SPRING
AVERAGE/LONG DISPLAY
HT: TO 1m/3ft/ROUNDED-SPREADING

Shrubby evergreens from South Africa, the 60-odd
Euryops species are grown in temperate climates and
are hardy down to −2°C/28°F. All are rather similar
except in minor botanical details. Their habit of
growth is rather sprawling, and a certain amount of
pruning after bloom helps keep them in some
semblance of shape. The alternately-borne leaves
are between 6 and 9cm in length, deeply lobed;
some species have a dark grey-green colouring,
others are covered with fine silver hair. The golden
daisy flowers appear singly on long stems and cut
well for small bouquets. A gravelly, well-drained soil
suits best, with ample water in dry weather. Propagate from short, semi-hardwood cuttings struck in
late autumn, with heat.

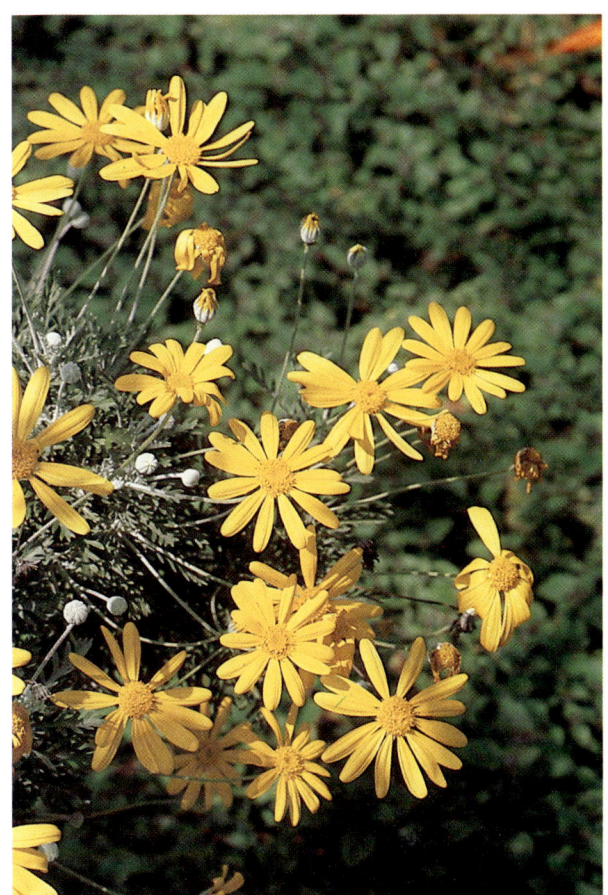

EURYOPS pectinatus
Yellow Marguerite

EXOCHORDA

Pearl Bush

SPRING
AVERAGE/SHORT DISPLAY
HT: 3-3.6m/10-12ft/SPARSE

This very small genus of the rose family includes
only four species, all from northern Asia, all surpas-
singly lovely. Considering their ease of propagation,
it is surprising they are not seen more often—but
then they dislike humid summers. You can raise
them from spring-sown seed, kept warm and moist,
or from semi-hardwood cuttings taken in autumn
and misted regularly, even by separating and potting
up suckers. They prefer a rich, well-drained soil, and
should be kept constantly moist except in cold
weather. They are deciduous, and the lightly
toothed ovate leaves produce a delicate display of
autumn colour. *Exochorda racemosa* bears terminal
racemes of snowy white 4cm flowers that are said to
look like a string of pearls in bud. Cut flower stems
lavishly to control shape and size.

EXOCHORDA racemosa
Pearl Bush

FEIJOA

Pineapple Guava,
Fruit Salad Plant

☼ ☀
T

SPRING
AVERAGE/LONG DISPLAY
HT: TO 4m/13ft/GLOBOSE OR TREE-LIKE

Not a true Guava, *Feijoa sellowiana* is nevertheless related, and produces a popular autumn fruit in the cooler climates. It is reported to reach small tree size in southern England, but in Australia seems content to remain as a rounded shrub. It needs a rich, well-drained soil and ample water in a dry summer to develop the ovoid, 5cm green fruit, which have a tangy, guava-like taste when ripe. The 7cm shiny leaves are oval, have woolly reverses. The decorative 4cm flowers are borne in pairs at the base of new season's growth. They have white, reflexed petals and a mass of deep red stamens. Propagate from seed or semi-hardwood cuttings in autumn. Strike them with heat and moisture.

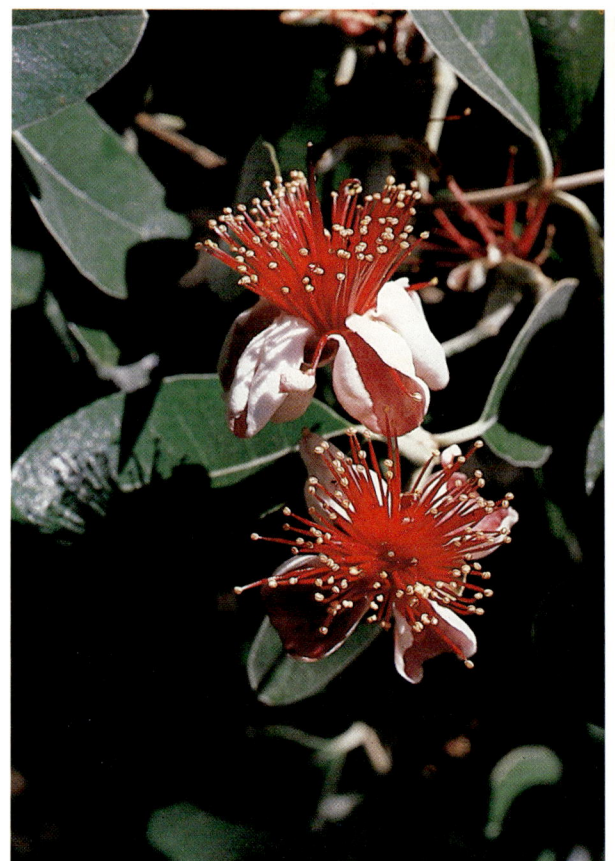

Feijoa sellowiana
Pineapple Guava

FELICIA
(syn AGATHAEA)

Blue Marguerite,
Blue Daisy

☼ T

SPRING–SUMMER
FAST/LONG DISPLAY
HT: 50cm/20in/LOW, SPREADING

Felicias add much sought-after blue and mauve to the spectrum of daisy flowers. Best known of some 50 African species is the Blue Marguerite, *F. amelloides*, a sturdy little plant that grows so fast in temperate climates it is often treated as a bedding plant and grown afresh from soft tip-cuttings at any time. It can also be raised from seed, which will germinate in a month at a temperature of 13°C/55°F. A low, generally tidy shrublet, it makes a brilliant warm weather display in rock gardens, as a path edging, or by the seaside. It is also useful in hillside gardens, and is hardy down to −3°C/27°F. The 2.5cm evergreen leaves are glossy and slenderly oval, the showy bright-blue flowers are borne at tip ends and cut well for posies. They have brilliantly gold disc centres.

FELICIA amelloides
Blue Marguerite

FORSYTHIA suspensa 'Sieboldii'
Weeping Forsythia

FORSYTHIA

Golden Bells

SPRING
AVERAGE/LONG DISPLAY
HT: 1.2-4m/4-13ft/FOUNTAIN SHAPED

Hardy down to −8°C/17°F, the beautiful golden-flowered *Forsythias* light up cold-climate gardens at the first breath of spring, their slender branches arching with the sheer weight of blossom. Like the early-blooming Japonicas (see *Chaenomeles*), their bare, budded stems will open indoors in plain water. Easy to grow in rich, well-drained soil, they are also easy to propagate, either from divisions or from semi-hardwood tip-cuttings taken in summer and struck in a cool, humid place. *F. suspensa* is conveniently self-layering, and well-rooted layers may be severed and lifted in late winter. *Forsythia* species don't like sub-tropical conditions at all, and should be tried only where the winters are cold, the summers dry (though they'll need heavy watering to keep growing). Quite deciduous, the coarsely toothed leaves are between 5 and 10cm in length. The open bell-shaped flowers appear in small clusters from lateral buds of the previous year's wood.

FORSYTHIA X intermedia
Golden Bells

FUCHSIA

Ladies' Eardrops

SPRING–AUTUMN
FAST/LONG DISPLAY
HT: 60-200cm/2-6ft/UPRIGHT–BUSHY

Driving in western County Cork on a recent visit to Ireland, I couldn't believe my eyes—those scarlet-blooming hedges were actually thickets of *Fuchsia*, arching over the roads, blooming riotously in every hedgerow during the Irish summer! The climate of southern Ireland is their ideal. Warmed by the Gulf Stream, it has humid summers and frost-free winters. Frequent mists and cloudy skies raise the humidity, soft rains drench the plants at any time of year. Fuchsias will grow in almost any soil, provided it contains plenty of organic matter and is not too acid. If your Azaleas bloom beautifully, better add half a cup of dolomite to the square metre for *Fuchsias* and feed them regularly with bone meal. They have a terrible thirst too. Water deeply and often, but never while the sun is directly on the plant. They will grow best among other shade-loving shrubs in the shelter of deciduous trees. In hot, dry areas, raise them in containers in a lath or

FUCHSIA X 'Mrs Popple'

FUCHSIA X 'King's Ransom'

FUCHSIA X 'Princess Dollar'

shade house and keep the humidity high. Varieties with a weeping habit make elegant basket plants in a sheltered position; those with stronger, upright growth can be trained as standards or espaliers. They even make showy (if temporary) indoor plants, but suffer from the dry indoor atmosphere. Raise them outside, in the shade, and bring inside for a few days only when they are in full bloom—which they mostly are from midsummer to autumn. Prune while they are dormant in late winter, and begin pinching back new shoots in spring for a compact, bushy habit and more flowers. New plants are easily raised from soft tip cuttings of 2 to 4 nodes, taken from late spring through autumn. Strike them in a warm, humid place. All *Fuchsias* have toothed, glossy foliage (mostly deciduous), and bear single flowers at leaf axils, most heavily at the ends of arching branches. Each bloom, drooping on a slender stem, consists of four reflexed sepals and four or more petals, frequently in a contrasting colour. The hybrids of *F. triphylla* are more suited to full sun, and bloom well in the semi-tropics.

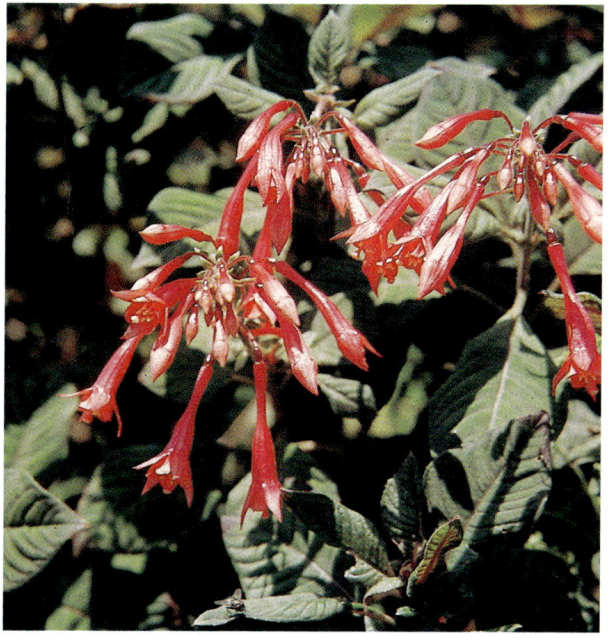

FUCHSIA triphylla
'Gartenmeister Bonstedt'

GALPHIMIA
(syn THRYALLIS)

Rain of Gold,
Rama de Oro,
Mexican Gold Bush

SUMMER
FAST/LONG DISPLAY
HT: 2m/7ft/ERECT

The charming popular name of this showy Mexican shrub is an understatement. On a mature specimen in full flower, the red stems are literally weighed down by terminal spikes of tiny golden star-flowers for weeks at a time. Individual blossoms fall after a day, and soon the ground for yards around turns to vivid yellow. Strictly a subject for the warm-temperate to tropical climate, it needs rich, well-drained soil and regular water to keep its roots damp. The opposite leaves are ovate, shiny and about 5cm in length; they are evergreen. Propagation can be undertaken from seed, or from cuttings of ripe wood, struck in a sharp, sandy mix with warmth and humidity. It can be clipped as a hedge plant.

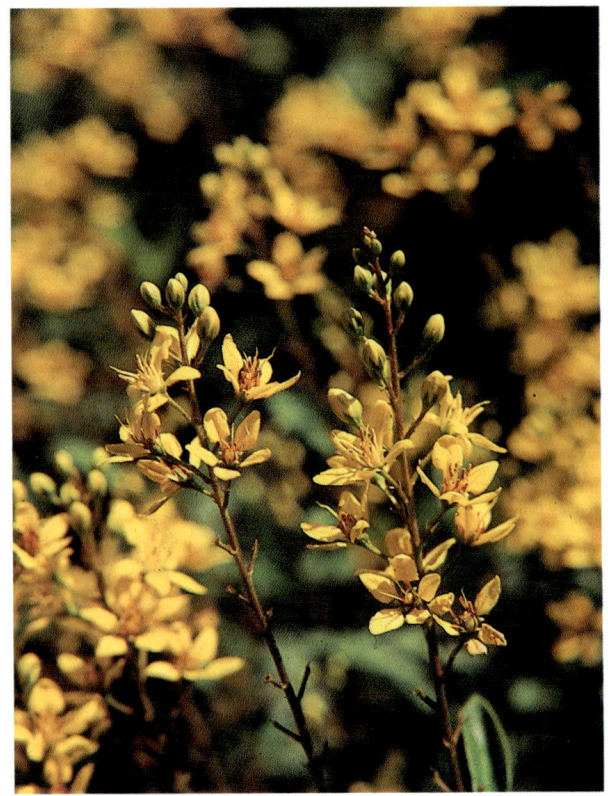

GALPHIMIA *glauca*
'Rain of Gold'

GAMOLEPIS

Paris Daisy

ALL YEAR
VERY FAST/LONG DISPLAY
HT: 1-1.8m/4-6ft/ROUNDED

An untidy shrub that needs regular pinching and pruning to maintain any sort of shape, *Gamolepis chrysanthemoides* is virtually indestructible, resists frost and drought to produce bursts of gay yellow daisy flowers all year. It is one of 10 species, all native to South Africa, and strongly resembling *Euryops* (which see) to all except the trained taxonomist. It seems to thrive in any soil, but of course does best in a leaf-rich, fast-draining loam with year-round water. The alternate leaves are bright green, deeply toothed and glossy, the long-stemmed daisy flowers yellow with a deeper gold eye. These pick well for small arrangements. Dead-heading of faded blooms is advisable to prevent the shrubs self-seeding everywhere. Don't worry about propagation, *Gamolepis* takes care of that without your help.

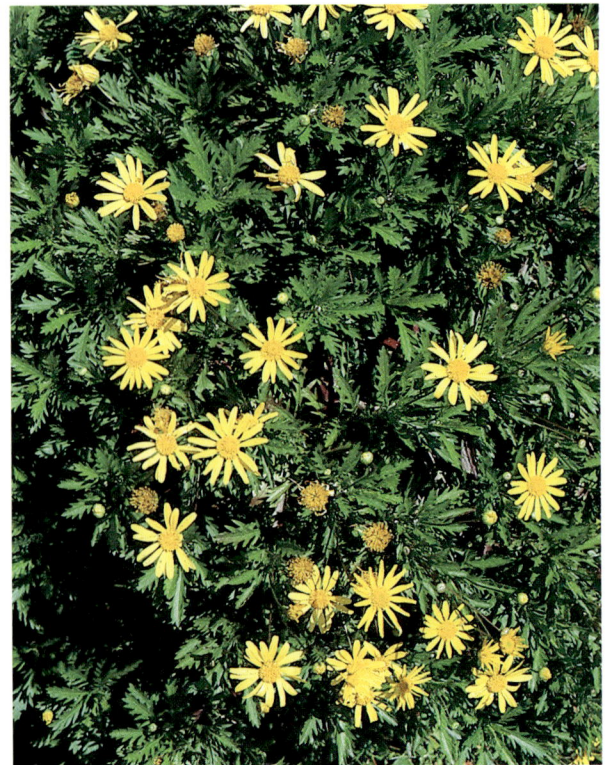

GAMOLEPIS *chrysanthemoides*
Paris Daisy

GARDENIA

FRAGRANT

Cape Jasmine,
Tiare

SPRING–SUMMER/ALL YEAR IN TROPICS
AVERAGE/INTERMITTENT DISPLAY
HT: 50-300cm/20-120in

Gardenias are cherished in every part of the world for their perfume, their snowy-white perfection. Though native to hot climates, they bloom where it is temperate in a sheltered position. Temperatures of from 5° to 9°C are not uncommon where I live, for instance, and I enjoy them for most of the year. They love humidity it is true, so I spray the foliage regularly and have planted them near a garden pool. A rich, well-drained, acid soil is best, and they are easily raised from 5-8cm semi-hardwood cuttings, taken with a heel in the cooler months. At this stage, they do strike better with warmth and humidity. Most commonly seen varieties are cultivars of *G. augusta:* 'Radicans' is a dwarf with 2.5cm flowers; 'Florida' has 7.5cm blooms; 'Professor Pucci' asymmetrical flowers to 12.5cm. Picking blooms is usually sufficient pruning for all types.

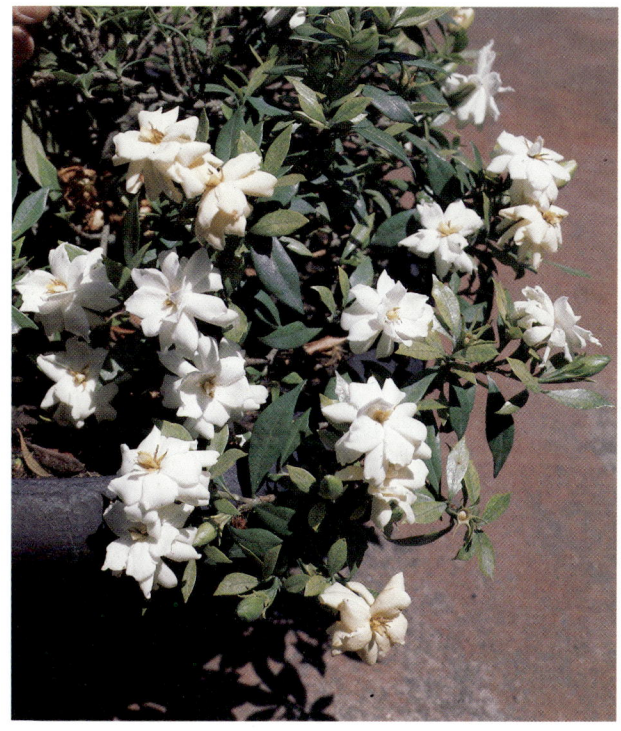

GARDENIA augusta 'Radicans'
Cape Jasmine

GARDENIA augusta 'Florida'
Florist's Gardenia

GARDENIA tahitiensis
Tiare

GARDENIA X 'Professor Pucci'
Giant Gardenia

GARDENIA thunbergii
Star Gardenia

GENISTA
(syn SPARTIUM)

FRAGRANT

Genet,
Broom,
Dyer's Greenweed

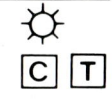

SUMMER
AVERAGE/LONG DISPLAY
HT: 30-100cm/1-3ft/SPREADING

Valued all around the temperate world for the brilliance of their golden pea-flowers, most species of *Genista* are native to the Mediterranean area. They are very sturdy plants, revelling in hot weather but surprisingly hardy in the cold, suffering damage only in prolonged freezes. They thrive by the sea, bloom their heads off in dry, drought-stricken areas, romp in a well-drained soil. Grow them from seed sown in spring after a 24 hour soak in warm water, or propagate from 10cm cuttings of semi-hardened wood taken with a heel in late summer. They are many-branched plants, sparsely foliaged even in the growing season. The deciduous leaves are narrow, sometimes needle-like. The golden flowers are massed in terminal racemes. All 75 species are tip-pruned to encourage bushiness.

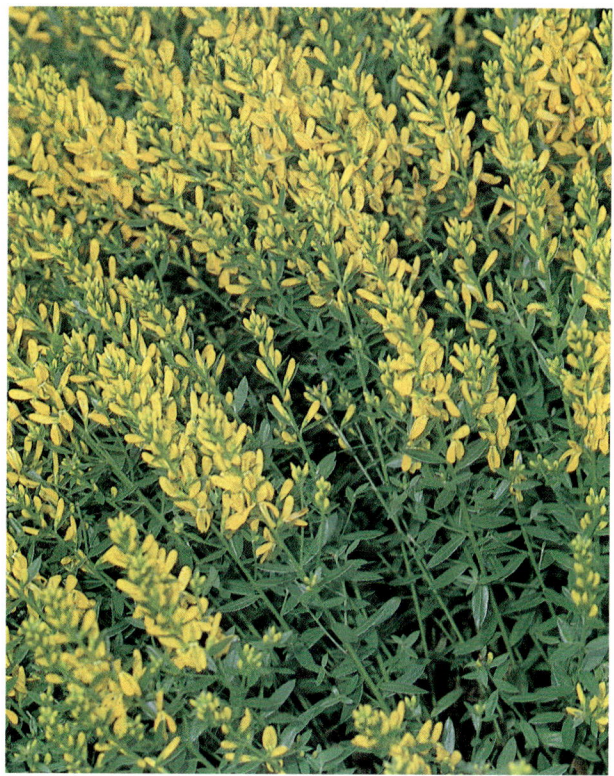

GENISTA tinctoria
Dyer's Greenweed

GENISTA hispanica
Spanish Broom

GREVILLEA X 'Robyn Gordon'

GREVILLEA

Spider Flowers

WINTER–SUMMER
AVERAGE/LONG DISPLAY
HT: 25-400cm/10-150in/VARIABLE

No apology to overseas readers should be needed for devoting so much precious space to this exclusively Australian genus. Most attractive and floriferous of the antipodean shrub genera, *Grevilleas* are also the most improved, having long attracted the attention of hybridists. Now, they bloom in a rainbow of colours, often for much of the year. California gardeners have discovered them in a big way, they are grown in Africa, New Zealand, all around the Mediterranean. In a word, they have caught the imagination of modern gardeners just as they once did the early plant hunters of the southern hemisphere. Variable in flower, foliage and habit, it is hardly surprising to learn they are members of the botanical family Proteaceae, named for the demigod Proteus, who could change his shape at will. Thus they are included with many other plants of bizarre appearance found exclusively in Australia, South Africa and South America, offering some proof of a prehistoric continental connection. *Grevilleas* are indeed so variable that it is hard to describe them as a group. But they seem to prefer full sun and grow best in a well-drained soil that is rich in leaf-mould and somewhat gravelly. It must also be slightly acid and on the dryish side—species from inland Australia in particular abhor humidity. *Grevilleas* appreciate a light ration of balanced fertilizer from time to time. An excess of phosphorus can result in very unhappy plants. While they can be grown from seed provided it is absolutely fresh, the preferred method of propagation is from firm tip-cuttings taken in late summer. These should be treated with a rooting hormone and set in a fast-draining sand/peat mixture. Warmth and humidity at this stage will promote rooting in no time. They

GREVILLEA X 'Sandra Gordon'

GREVILLEA X 'Canberra Gem'

GREVILLEA ilicifolia
Holly Grevillea

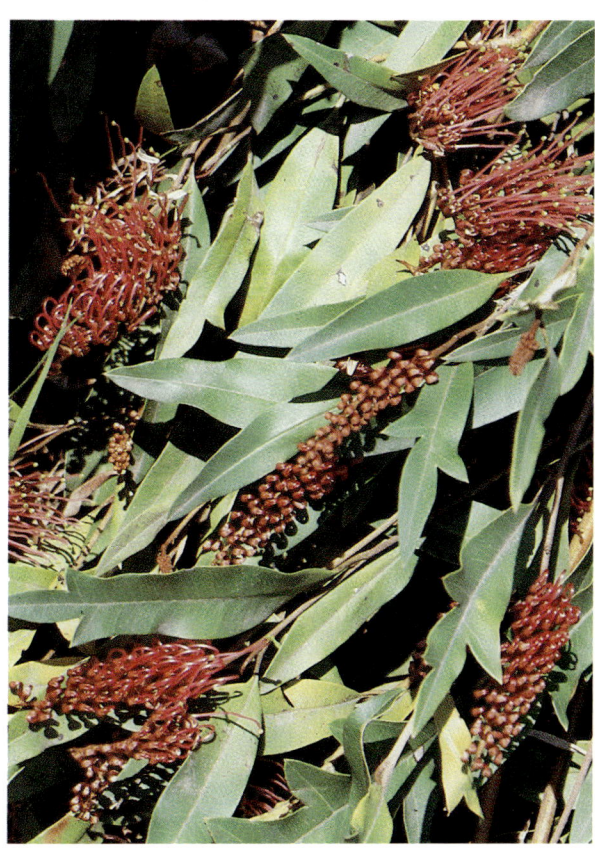

GREVILLEA X 'Poorinda Royal Mantle'

can also be grafted, and the illustrated G. X 'Poorinda Royal Mantle' makes a splendid weeping feature when grafted onto a tall stock of the tree species G. *robusta*. Of the illustrated cultivars, G. X 'Robyn Gordon' is far and away the most popular, and moderately frost hardy. It is a low, spreading plant with deeply divided leaves and arching sprays of scarlet bloom borne much of the year. These resemble one of its parents, the tree species G. *banksii*. Its stable mate G. X 'Sandra Gordon' is an interspecific hybrid of tall, open habit with similar foliage and golden-yellow flower spikes. It grows to 4m. G. X 'Canberra Gem' is a densely-branched hybrid between the species G. *rosmarinifolia* and G. *juniperina*. It is hardy down to −8°C/17°F. G. *ilicifolia* varies from upright to spreading. Its blooms are one-sided, deep red, and its foliage resembles holly. G. X 'Poorinda Royal Mantle' is a widely spreading ground cover, rarely more than 25cm high, but spanning as wide as 7m. West Australian G. *biternata* is also used for ground cover, growing to about 50cm high and bearing clouds of white, perfumed flowers in spring. Random, upright branches should be pruned away. Finally, G. *lavandulacea*, a most variable plant according to its locality, but often less than 1m high. Its tiny, lavender-like leaves form a dense background to hanging, spidery blooms in many shades. All *Grevilleas* are attractive to birds, particularly honey-eaters. There are over 200 natural species, all of them lovely. If you must prune them, do it with a light hand.

GREVILLEA *biternata*
Woolly Grevillea

GREVILLEA *lavandulacea*
Lavender Grevillea

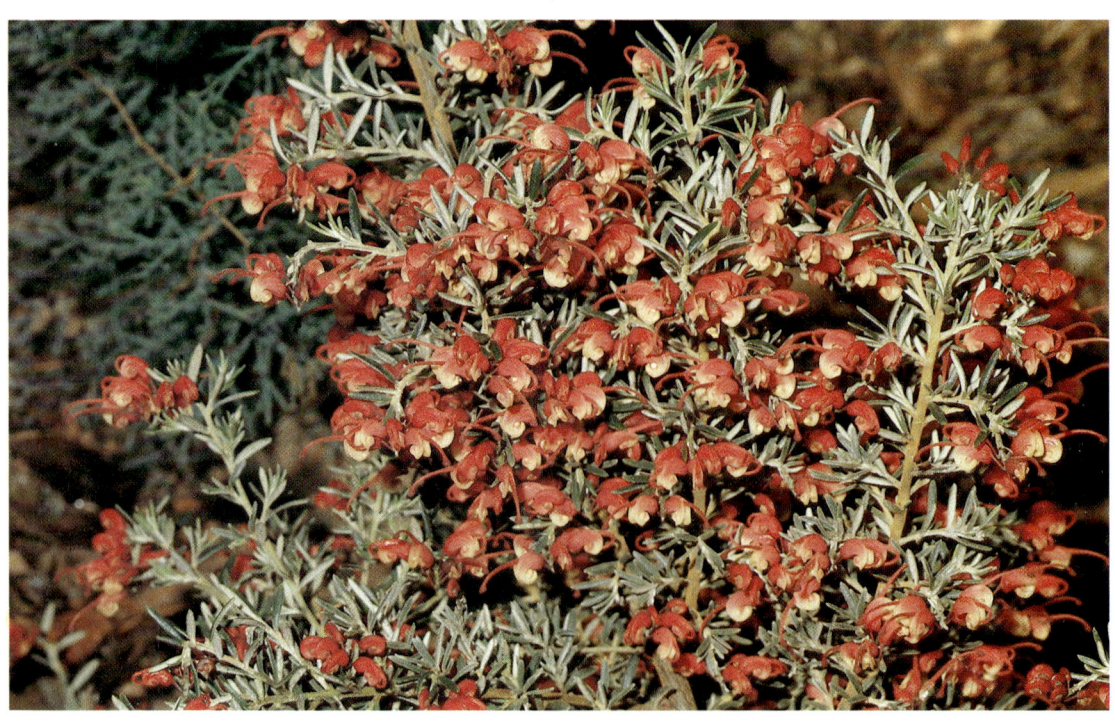

GREYIA

Mountain Bottlebrush,
Baakhout

WINTER–SPRING
SLOW/LONG DISPLAY
HT: 50-250cm/4½-8ft/SPRAWLING

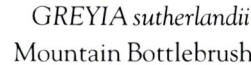

A small South African genus, *Greyia* was named for a one-time Governor of the Cape. All 3 species are hardy to occasional frost, but need protection where the winters are really cold. They prefer a dry, fast-draining soil and should be watered sparingly except in summer, their principal growth season. Grow them from seed (if you can get it) or from cuttings of half-ripened wood struck under glass. They do best in hot, exposed positions such as large rockeries, but often adopt a sprawling habit. The semi-deciduous leaves resemble those of the edible fig and cluster at branch tips, where the spectacular orange-red inflorescences appear any time in winter and spring. In late autumn, many of the leaves may colour before falling.

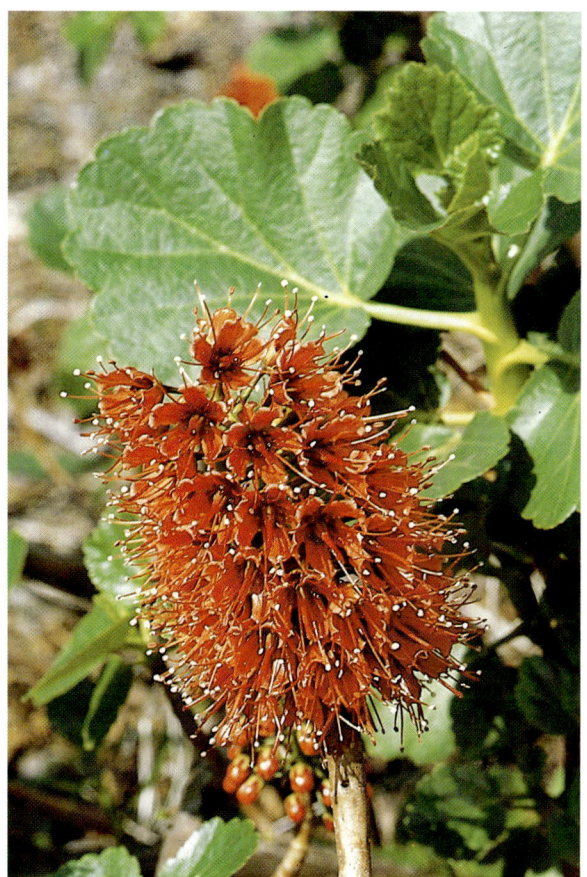

GREYIA sutherlandii
Mountain Bottlebrush

HAMAMELIS   FRAGRANT

Witch Hazel,
Chinese Witch Hazel

WINTER
SLOW/SHORT DISPLAY
HT: 2.5-4m/8-14ft

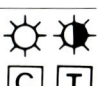

Stunning in winter flower arrangements, the strap-like golden petals of Chinese Witch Hazel resist frost and icy winds to drape the bare zig-zag branches all through the cold months. Grow them among deciduous trees where winter sunlight can reach, but choose a well-drained acid soil, enriched with plenty of leaf-mould. *Hamamelis mollis* is from China, spreads slowly into a sparsely furnished bush clothed with 13cm leaves that are widest near the tips. They are coarsely toothed and deciduous. Branches of the winter blossom may be cut in bud, will spread a charming fragrance indoors. Seed is very slow to germinate; best propagate from 10cm heeled cuttings taken in autumn.

HAMAMELIS mollis
Chinese Witch Hazel

HEBE salicifolia
Koromiko

HEBE

Veronica,
Shrub Speedwell,
New Zealand Lilac,
Koromiko

☼ ☀
T

WINTER–SUMMER
FAST/LONG DISPLAY
HT: 15-500cm/6in-15ft/COMPACT

A diverse shrub genus for the cool temperate garden, *Hebe* includes some 80 natural species, mostly native to New Zealand. They are evergreen, and do best in the frost-free coastal garden as thick groundcovers, in massed shrubberies or trimmed as dense hedges. Commonly planted garden types are mostly cultivars which can be propagated only by means of cuttings. These are taken in midsummer, trimmed to 10cm, inserted in a mixture of peat and sand in a cool place. When rooted (generally the following spring) they should be potted up individually, hardened outdoors and finally planted in a permanent position in early autumn. *Hebes* are not

HEBE X 'Inspiration'
New Zealand Lilac

HEBE speciosa 'Hidcote'
Veronica

at all fussy as to soil (accepting even a little lime) and are remarkably maintenance-free. Most *Hebes* require no regular pruning, though there is no doubt an occasional shearing in earliest spring will improve their vigour. Take branches back to half their former length, feed over the root area and new growth will break from the cut twigs within a few days. Even pests are inclined to leave *Hebes* alone, only downy mildew causing much of a problem. All *Hebe* species and cultivars prefer a well-drained soil while liking plenty of air moisture—even moist salt air is acceptable, and they positively thrive in sheltered coastal gardens. Low growing types such as *H. cattaractae*, *H. pinguifolia* and *H. X 'Waikiki'* make decorative ground covers, for they normally grow less than 30cm/1ft in height and spread widely. Taller *H. buxifolia*, *H. elliptica*, *H. 'Inspiration'* and *H. salicifolia* can be clipped as dense hedges or rounded 'bun-shaped' specimens. Most *Hebes* have decorative, glossy, paired foliage with colourful new leaves. While blooming most heavily from late winter into summer, they may produce some spires of Veronica-like bloom at any time. Colours are white, blue, purple and cerise, some cultivars having attractive, variegated foliage. *Hebes* prefer minimum winter temperatures in the range of 5-7°C/40-45°F, but will withstand lower if trees provide overhead frost shelter. Hebe, the namesake of these lovely plants, by the way, was the goddess of youth in classical Greek mythology.

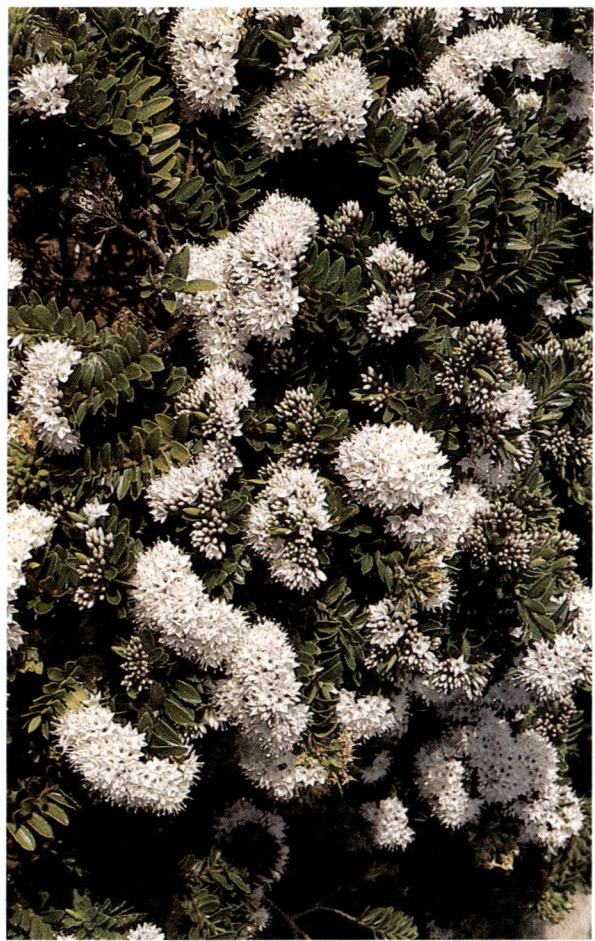

HEBE pinguifolia 'Pagei'
Shrub Speedwell

HIBISCUS insularis
Island Hibiscus

HIBISCUS

Rose of China,
Rose Mallow,
Rosella,
Rose of Sharon,
Shrub Althaea

SUMMER–AUTUMN
FAST/LONG DISPLAY
HT: 1-3.5m/3-12ft

☼
C T H

Pioneer botanist Linnaeus first used the name 'Rose of China' in the 18th century, when he christened these fantastic tropical flowers *Hibiscus rosa-sinensis.* He believed they came from China itself (they were certainly grown there at the time of the earliest European contacts) but modern botanical research suggests the Indian Ocean area as the most likely original home. Species sufficiently compatible to cross are found in East Africa, Malagasy and Malaysia, and also throughout the Pacific islands. Other species, native to the Middle East and China itself, do not cross with *H. rosa-sinensis.* At any rate, these Roses of China reach their full glory only in

HIBISCUS calyphyllus

HIBISCUS *rosa-sinensis*
Rose of China

HIBISCUS CV 'Elegance'

warm to tropical gardens. In really tropic zones, they bloom year round (in cooler areas in summer only), the flowers peaking in size at about 25cm diameter with the advent of autumn rains.

The spiritual if not the actual home of the ornamental *Hibiscus* is Hawaii, whose floral emblem it has become. The Hawaiian Islands have several native species and these have been crossed with at least 33 other species from different tropic areas to produce the stunning hybrids we know today. At one time, there were over 5000 named cultivars grown there, but the islanders became bored with them, and now reserve their enthusiasm for other flowers. *Hibiscus* species range all the way from small annuals to trees, but the most popular types, illustrated on these pages, are all shrubs. *H. syriacus* (which really does come from Syria) is a favourite in European and North American gardens. It has single and double varieties in shades of pink, white and mauve, often with a deep red blotch. It is not compatible with any of the others illustrated, but they will rarely be found in gardens with the same climate anyway. *H. calyphyllus* and *H. schizopetalus* are native to East Africa. *H. heterophyllus* grows naturally in north-east Australia. Uncommon *H. insularis* has been found only on Norfolk and Phillip Islands in the South Pacific but grows particularly well in coastal areas elsewhere. All are best propagated from 10cm cuttings taken in spring or summer and struck in a peat/sand mixture at a temperature of around 18°C/64°F.

HIBISCUS CV 'Cameo Queen'

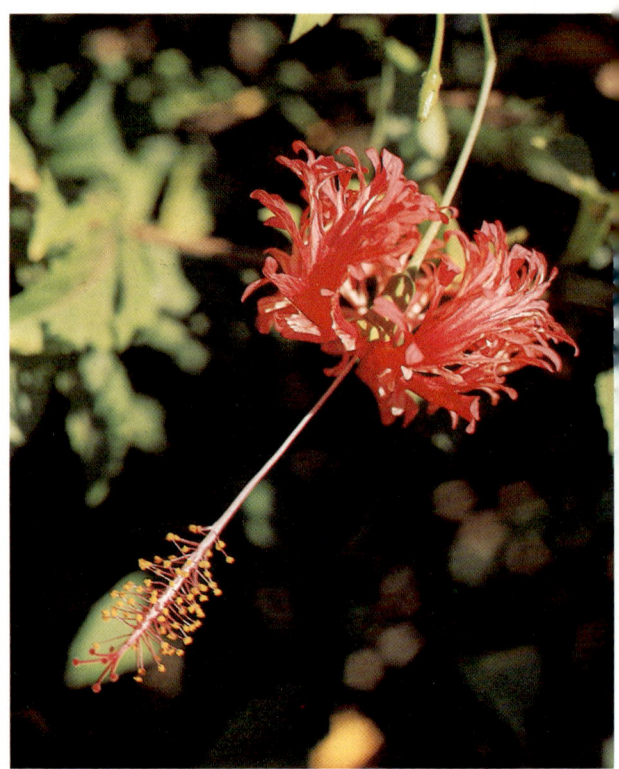

HIBISCUS syriacus 'Bluebird'
Rose of Sharon

HIBISCUS schizopetalus
Skeleton Hibiscus

HIBISCUS heterophyllus

HOLMSKIOLDIA sanguinea
Chinese Hat Plant

HOLMSKIOLDIA

Chinese Hat Plant,
Mandarin's Hat,
Cup and Saucer Plant

☼
T H

AUTUMN
FAST/LONG DISPLAY
HT: 3.5m/12ft/SPRAWLING

Named for an 18th century Danish botanist, this small genus has only one of its three species in cultivation. The Chinese Hat Plant, *Holmskioldia sanguinea* is rather untidy, making a considerable growth of slender branches that weep under their own weight. A single plant may spread much wider than its 3.5m height. The foliage is evergreen, consisting of dark ovate leaves, each about 10cm in length. The curious orange-scarlet flowers appear in autumn, clustered in dense terminal and axillary racemes. The flowers proper are tubular, but each is backed with a thin, disc-like calyx which really does resemble a Chinese hat. A mature plant of *Holmskioldia* may be kept vigorous with a light annual pruning. This is best done by eliminating several of the oldest canes entirely. Poor but well-drained soil is satisfactory. Propagation is from semi-hardened tip-cuttings struck with heat in spring or summer. Altogether a spectacular and exciting plant, but only for the warmer climate garden or heated glasshouse elsewhere.

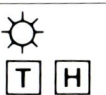

HOLMSKIOLDIA sanguinea
'Lucidum'

HYDRANGEA macrophylla
Hortensia

HYDRANGEA

Hortensia,
Hills of Snow,
Lacecap,
PeeGee

SUMMER–AUTUMN
FAST/LONG DISPLAY
HT: 1-4.5m/3-15ft

Favourite shrubs for the large, shaded border or sun-less aspect, *Hydrangeas* produce big, showy flowerheads in midsummer, and are often used for Christmas decorations in the southern hemisphere. There are over 30 deciduous species, from China, Japan and North America, and one evergreen species, *H. integerrima*, which hails from Chile and generally develops a climbing habit. All enjoy deep, porous soil and ample water, making massive growth in the warmer months. Their terrible thirst is clearly indicated by their botanical name, which is adapted from the Greek *hydor aggeion* or 'water vessel'. *Hydrangeas* of all types can be planted in autumn or early spring. They need overhead shelter from frost in colder areas, and look better in a position where morning sun cannot damage damp foliage. All species do best in semi-shade, except in generally cloudy areas, where full sun is readily accepted.

The most commonly grown species is *H. macrophylla* from China and Japan. It has many flower forms, which must be propagated from cuttings to come true, and have one very striking peculiarity. While they do equally well in acid or alkaline soil, their colour is quite changeable. Generally mauve or blue in acid soils, in alkaline they become pink or red. And it is possible to switch from one colour range to the other by repeated chemical additions to the soil. Aluminium sulphate turns them blue; lime turns them pink, it is as simple as that. But there are also white and greenish varieties which rarely tone at all. All *macrophylla* Hydrangeas have two sorts of flower: one tiny and fertile with minute petals surrounding a cluster of stamens, the other sterile, with large, showy sepals and no stamens at all. Varieties consisting almost entirely of the sterile florets are known as 'Hortensias' and are most commonly sought after. Heads with a large proportion of fertile

HYDRANGEA arborescens
Hills of Snow

HYDRANGEA macrophylla
'Parsifal' Hydrangea

florets are known as 'Lacecaps'. Both types are pruned heavily during late winter, cutting each cane back to a pair of plump growth buds. The ultimate size of each bush can be controlled in this way.

The second most popular *Hydrangea* species are the PeeGee types, *H. paniculata grandiflora*, which grow taller than the *macrophyllas* (to 5m) and bear terminal panicles of white bloom up to 45cm in length. These are greenish at first, gradually fading to pink. Rarely seen in the southern hemisphere is climbing *H. petiolaris* which can scale a rough-barked tree or textured wall to produce flat heads of creamy-white blossom in summer. All *hydrangeas* may be propagated from 15cm cuttings of unflowered shoots taken in early autumn. These should be struck in a peat/sand mixture preferably over heat, and planted out the following autumn. Keep watch for aphids and red spider-mites which can defoliate entire plants where the air is dry. In cold winter areas, both flowers and foliage of some *Hydrangea* varieties may turn gorgeous shades of red, green or rust, and make wonderful indoor displays.

HYDRANGEA aspera

HYDRANGEA macrophylla normalis
Lacecap Hydrangea

HYDRANGEA macrophylla

HYDRANGEA paniculata
Pee Gee Hydrangea

HYPERICUM

St John's Wort,
Aaron's Beard,
Goldflower,
Rose of Sharon

SPRING–AUTUMN
AVERAGE/LONG DISPLAY
HT: 15-150cm/6-60in/SPREADING

This wonderfully showy genus is represented in the wild on every continent, mostly in the form of shrubs. Sometimes evergreen, sometimes deciduous, they provide year-round colour in a mild temperate climate and are easy to grow. Full sun is a must for at least part of each day, and a fast-draining soil will give good results. Set out in either autumn or spring (but preferably the latter) in enriched, deeply dug soil, and give the roots a winter protection of deep mulch. Small species should be propagated from 5cm cuttings taken in late spring. Taller varieties grow best from 12.5cm summer cuttings of non-flowering shoots. Both types are set out in their

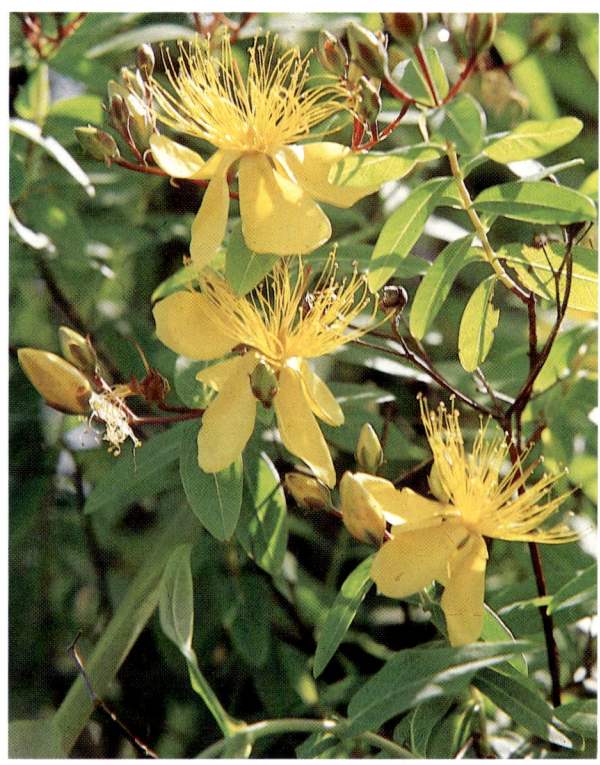

HYPERICUM chinense
St John's Wort

HYPERICUM patulum

HYPERICUM X 'Rowallane'
Rose of Sharon

final position when well-rooted, about 10 months later. All species need annual pruning to maintain shape, and it is customary to cut them back to within a few shoots of old wood during winter. Pests do not seem to be a bother, but leaves are occasionally attacked by rust and should be sprayed with a fungicide when this occurs.

Between 300 and 400 *Hypericum* species are recognized, with the most spectacular blooms being found, among the cultivars. Those of illustrated 'Rowallane' may be 7.5cm in diameter. Smaller flowered *H. inodorum* makes the best mass display, while dwarf-growing *H. cerastoides* (syn *H. rhodopaeum*) is a showy plant in rock gardens or at the front of the mixed border. Seed pods should be removed from all species to maintain vigour.

HYPERICUM cerastoides
Prostrate Goldflower

HYPERICUM inodorum
Goldflower

IBOZA
(syn MOSCHOSMA)

Nutmeg Bush,
Misty Plume Bush

☼ T

WINTER
FAST/LONG DISPLAY
HT: TO 2m/7ft

Softly-flowered, spicily scented, the tender South African *Iboza riparia* is one of around a dozen species in a decorative genus of the mint family. It is of particular value in a mild coastal climate, where the entire bush bursts into bloom in midwinter. Cuttings struck in early spring will flower the following winter, so fast is its growth. The shrubs are almost completely deciduous, with toothed, velvety leaves developing as bloom fades. The tiny silvery-pink flowers are sprinkled with purple anthers and appear in long terminal panicles. Hard pruning is necessary to maintain shape, and up to three-quarters of the previous season's growth should be removed.

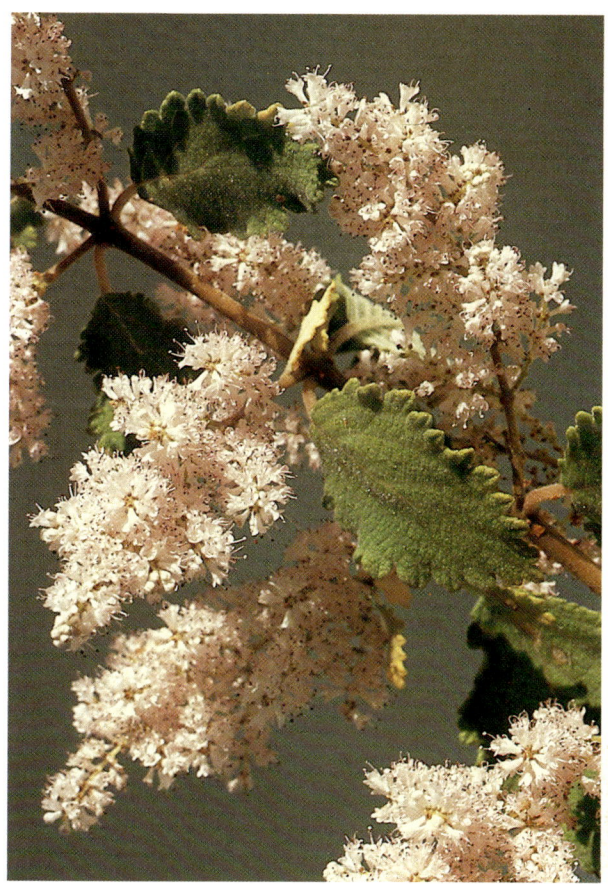

IBOZA riparia
Nutmeg Bush

IOCHROMA

Tubeflower

☼
T H

SUMMER–AUTUMN
FAST/LONG DISPLAY
HT: TO 3m/10ft/SPREADING

Long tubular flowers, mostly in shades of purple, hang all summer long on these fast-growing shrubs, of which about 20 species are grown. *Iochromas* are easily raised from cuttings and grow best in a warm, sheltered spot with plenty of water. As summer hots up, they will send out succulent stems and felty 20cm leaves, quickly becoming untidy and straggly unless kept in shape. Try them as a wall shrub or espalier for maximum display value, and plant in a sheltered spot for protection against winds. *I. grandiflora*, *I. lanceolata* and *I. tubulosa* bloom in varying shades of purple. *I. coccinea* is scarlet, *I. flava* a pale yellow. *I. fuchsioides* has a broader flower, tinted a rich orange-scarlet.

IOCHROMA tubulosa
Violet Tubeflower

ISOPOGON

Coneflower,
Drumsticks,
Conebush

WINTER–SPRING
AVERAGE/LONG DISPLAY
HT: 1-2m/3-7ft/SPREADING

Less well-known than other members of the Protea family outside their native Australia, the 30-odd species of *Isopogon* are found mostly on the west coast, but with several useful representatives in the east. They like an acid, sandy soil, with regular water in the growing season, and have been cultivated successfully in California, the Mediterranean area and England's Scilly Isles. All produce cone-shaped flower heads from winter on, and have stiff, needle-like foliage. The blooms vary in colour from yellow to pink, purple and white. They cut well and are useful for bulking large arrangements. Propagate from well-ripened seed in winter or early spring, or from cuttings struck in sharp sand and peat.

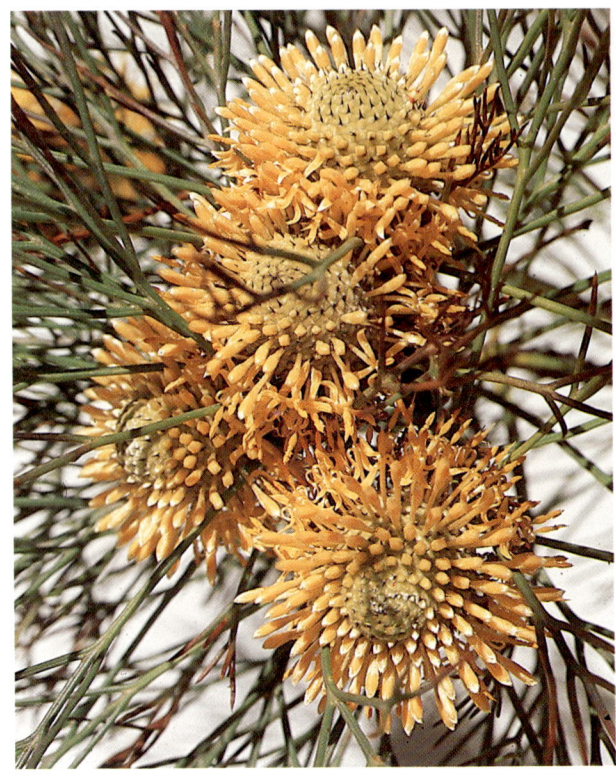

ISOPOGON *anethifolius*
Drumsticks

ISOPOGON *dubius*
Rosy Coneflower

IXORA

Jungle Flame,
Jungle Geranium

SUMMER–AUTUMN
FAST/LONG DISPLAY
HT: 1-2m/3-7ft/SPREADING

Colourful shrubs from all over South-east Asia, Africa and the Pacific Islands, *Ixoras* are related to Gardenias and many other tropical favourites. Admirably suited to their popular name of Jungle Flame, they are striking plants for gardens where the humidity is high. Grow them in a sandy soil rich with leaf-mould, and give plenty of moisture throughout the summer. Cut back to shape in winter, when they may be allowed to dry out a little. *Ixora chinensis* 'Prince of Orange' is often used as a mass bedding plant in the tropics, but the flowers fade badly, and it is more brilliant in semi-shade. The larger-growing *I. coccinea* or Jungle Geranium is a handsome shrub with golden-green foliage and large heads of deep scarlet bloom. Propagate from spring cuttings struck over heat.

IXORA coccinea
Jungle Geranium

IXORA chinensis
Jungle Flame

JASMINUM

Jasmine,
Jessamine,
Pikake,
Pitate

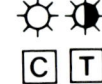

SPRING–WINTER
FAST/ALL SEASON
HT: 1-3.6m/3-12ft

Think of fragrance—think of Jasmine! Delicate
starry flowers in yellow, white or pink according to
species, and native to all the fabled lands of the East.
You can have Jasmine scenting your house and
garden the whole year round if you pick the right
species from among the 20-odd listed by taxonomists. Just give them a partially shaded or sunny position, reasonable soil, a regular ration of water and
watch them take off. You can choose dwarf types for
the rock garden or ground cover, vining and twining

JASMINUM mesneyi
Primrose Jasmine

JASMINUM azoricum
Lemon-scented Jasmine

JASMINUM fruticans
Yellow Jasmine

JASMINUM nudiflorum
Winter Jasmine

JASMINUM sambac
Arabian Jasmine, Pikake

varieties to cover a fence or pergola, and dense or compact growers that look best as a specimen shrub. They'll need a regular going over with the secateurs to keep them in bounds though, for almost all Jasmines love to turn climber if you let them have their heads.

Jasminum nudiflorum is the first to bloom, opening simple 1cm flowers from its bare twigs in the winter sunlight. In its native Japan they call it 'the Flower that Welcomes Spring'. *J. mesneyi* (with much larger semi-double golden blooms on arching canes) follows at the first sign of warm weather; and you'll know spring has truly arrived when pink-budded *J. polyanthum* bursts into bloom. It is strictly a climbing shrub, and will cover a wall in no time with light support. The Italian Jasmine, *J. officinale* and yellow-flowered *J. fruticans* keep up the fragrance throughout the summer, overlapping with *J. azoricum* which will bloom continuously till the following winter. In warmer climates, *J. sambac* will bloom intermittently throughout the warm weather. Almost all Jasmines are easy to propagate from 8cm cuttings of nearly ripe wood in summer; by layers; even from seed when it is produced.

JUSTICIA
(*syn JACOBINIA, CYRTANTHERA*)

Plume Flower,
Paradise Plant

SUMMER–AUTUMN
FAST/SHORT DISPLAY
HT: 1.5-3.5m/5-12ft

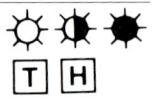

In the semi-tropical garden, or a shaded sunny aspect in frost-free areas, the showy South American Plume Flowers produces tall spikes of typical Acanthus bloom all through the summer. The colour range is wide—pink, red, orange, yellow and white—but the actual display is short. However, repeat flowering can be induced with well-drained acid soil, regular water and feeding. Prune back hard in early spring to encourage branching and large, handsome leaves; neglect makes them grow tall and scruffy. All species can be increased from 10cm cuttings of young growth taken in spring and potted up under heat of 21°C/70°F. Spray with systemic insecticide to prevent caterpillars making a mess of both flowers and foliage.

JUSTICIA aurea
King's Crown

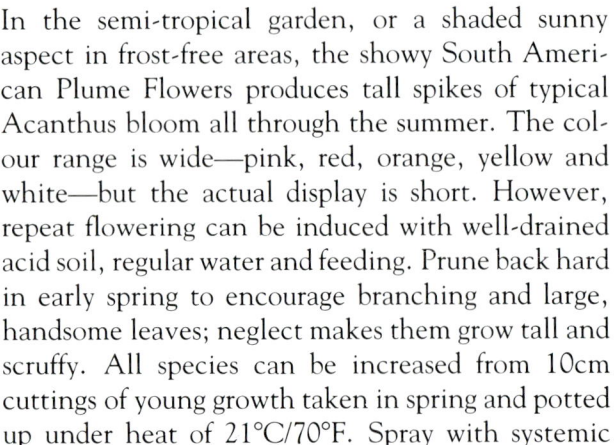

JUSTICIA carnea
Brazilian Plume Flower

KALMIA

 **FRAGRANT**

Mountain Laurel,
Calico Bush

☀
C T

SPRING–SUMMER
SLOW/LONG DISPLAY
HT: 1.8-3m/6-10ft/BROAD

Garden treasures away from their native American mountains, the slow-growing *Kalmias* are a small genus that enjoys exactly the same conditions as their Rhododendron relatives: part shade, humidity, an acid soil rich in leaf-mould. The laurel-like leaves are dark and glossy, the flowers (white, red or apple-blossom pink according to variety) have a curious sticky feel. *Kalmias* are completely cold-hardy and will survive below-zero temperatures. They are planted out in late spring or early autumn, and need no pruning beyond dead-heading. Best propagated by layering the current season's wood in late summer, they may also be struck from cuttings, though this is less reliable.

KALMIA latifolia
Mountain Laurel

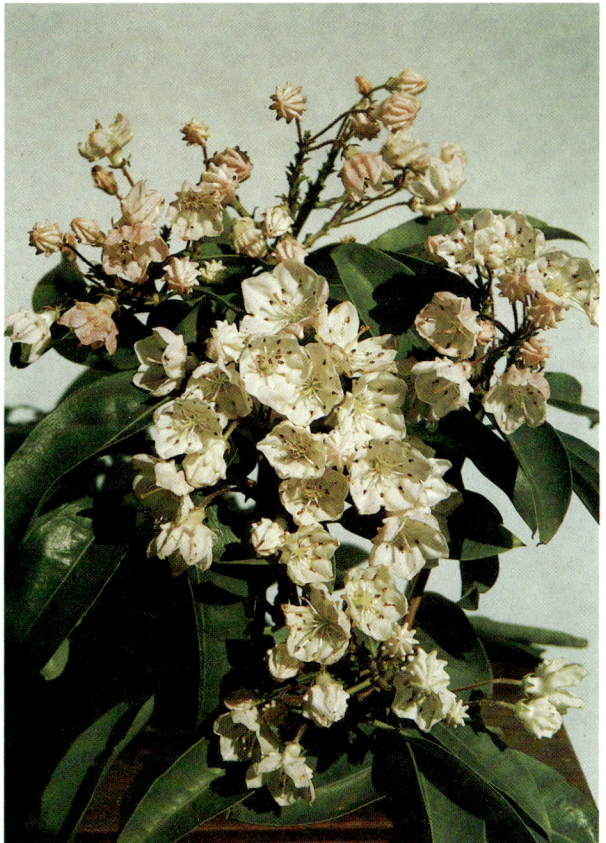

KALMIA latifolia (in bud)

99

KERRIA

Japanese Rose,
Jew's Mallow,
Globe Flower,
Bachelor's Button

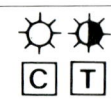

SPRING
FAST/LONG DISPLAY
HT: 1-1.8m/4-6ft/SUCKERING

A decorative deciduous member of the rose family, *Kerria* is the only species in its genus, and a great favourite in cooler climate gardens, where it lights up shaded corners with a profusion of golden spring blooms. Easily grown from cuttings, layers or divisions, it spreads rapidly and needs at least a 2m diameter space to display its graceful arching branches. These are festooned with doubly-toothed leaves from early spring and glow with autumn colour. The flowers (single or double in CV 'Pleniflora') cut well for indoor display. *Kerria* needs a rich, fast-draining soil and occasional heavy watering. It is frost hardy down to −6°C/21°F and needs a heavy pruning after flower-fall.

KERRIA japonica variegata
Japanese Rose

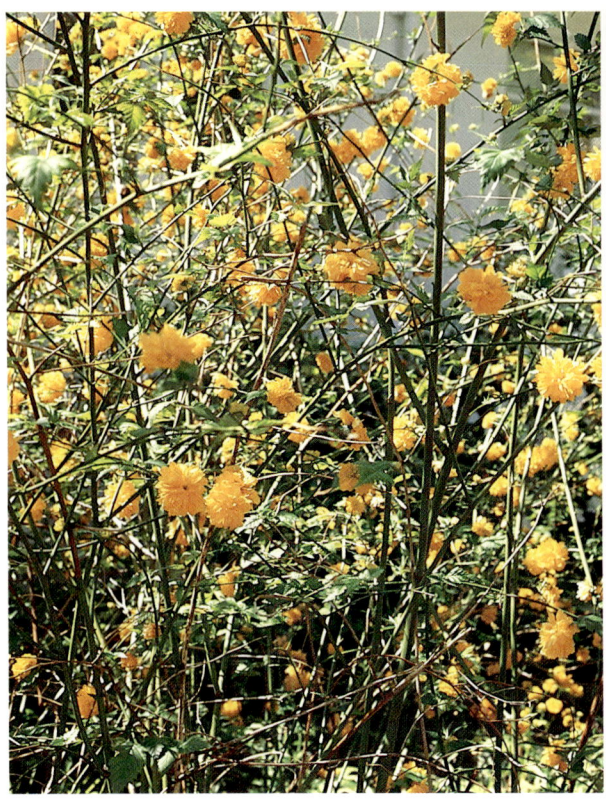

KERRIA japonica 'Pleniflora'
Bachelor's Buttons

KOLKWITZIA *amabilis*
Chinese Beauty Bush

KOLKWITZIA FRAGRANT

Beauty Bush

☼
C T

SPRING
FAST/LONG DISPLAY
HT: 2-3m/7-10ft/ARCHING

Related to Honeysuckle and to the Abelias (for which it is sometimes mistaken) the graceful Chinese Beauty Bush *Kolkwitzia amabilis* is surely one of the loveliest of garden plants. Grow it in a well-watered, sunny position with roots partially shaded—but allow plenty of room, for the tall, arching stems will soon grow to full height, draping themselves in spring with spicily fragrant masses of palest pink trumpet flowers, their throats spotted orange-yellow. *Kolkwitzia* is in every sense a year-round plant. When not in bloom it displays attractive winter bark, soft autumn leaf-colour and foliage that remains decorative throughout the summer. *Kolkwitzia* is commonly planted in late autumn or early spring in any good quality garden soil. It may be propagated from 15cm lateral cuttings taken with a heel in midsummer. These are struck in a sand/peat mixture in a coldframe, and are ready for setting out the following autumn. Prune out a selection of older flowering stems annually to keep mature bushes vigorous. Hardy down to −10°C/14°F.

LANTANA  AROMATIC

Shrub Verbena

SPRING–AUTUMN
FAST/ALL SEASON
HT: 1-3m/3-10ft/SPREADING

☼ T H

These splashy-flowered shrubs really do appear to be sprinkled with posies of tiny Verbena flowers in mixed or separate colours. Native mostly to the Americas, they have become a great favourite in mild winter areas, but many species can quickly become unwelcome guests. The cheery, mauve-flowered *Lantana sellowiana* is the exception—its dainty arched stems make a wonderful ground cover or small hedge and never become troublesome.

The more robust *L. camara* can quickly take over a whole garden if not pruned back regularly, and is already staking a claim to vast areas of Australia. In its specific pink-flowered form, it has been pro-claimed a noxious weed in many countries; it has largely been spread by birds, which excrete seed from the juicy black fruit. After all that, any help with its cultivation would seem quite unwelcome—but in fact there are many sterile hybrid forms of *L. camara* which are among the most useful of hedging shrubs in the warm climate garden. These must be propagated from 7.5cm cuttings, taken in summer and struck in sharp sand and peat at a temperature of 18°C/64°F. They should be pinched back several times as they grow to encourage bushiness, and set out early the following spring in their final positions. They need a temperature of at least 7°C to survive winter happily, and should be allowed almost to dry out over that season. Plenty of summer water is required, but too rich a soil makes the plants bolt to leaf rather than bloom. CV 'Cloth of Gold' is pure yellow; CV 'Nivea' white and yellow; CV 'Chelsea Gem' scarlet and yellow; CV 'Rose Queen' is pink and salmon yellow. Regular light tip-pruning gives best results.

LANTANA X 'Nivea'
White Lantana

LANTANA X 'Cloth of Gold'

LANTANA X 'Chelsea Gem'
Shrub Verbena

LANTANA sellowiana
Trailing Lantana

LAVANDULA spica
English Lavender

LAVANDULA FRAGRANT

Lavender

☼
C T

SPRING–SUMMER
FAST/ALL SEASON
HT: 30-100cm/1-3ft/SPREADING

French Lavender, English Lavender, Italian Laven-der, Dutch Lavender, Spanish Lavender—take your pick! But let it not be on nationalistic grounds, for all of the 20-30 species are native to the same area of the western Mediterranean. *Lavandula spica* is the mounded, silvery-leafed type with long-stemmed heads of bloom that are so easy to strip for sachets. The others tend to grow leggier, with shorter flower spikes. All are hardy down to −5°C/23°F, and none of them appreciate humidity. Propagate from autumn cuttings of ripened shoots with a heel and set out the following spring. Grow generally on the dryish side in light, gravelly soil. Deadhead regularly and prune lightly to keep compact.

LAVANDULA stoechas
Spanish Lavender

LEONOTIS

Lion's Tail,
Wild Dagga,
Lion's Ear

SUMMER–AUTUMN
FAST/ALL SEASON
HT: TO 2m/7ft

This small genus of perennials, shrubs and sub-shrubs hails almost exclusively from Africa, but one species, the shrubby *Leonotis leonurus*, has spread throughout the temperate world because of its great value as a garden feature plant. Tall and striking if kept well-groomed, it produces whorls or layers of velvety white or orange flowers right up the 2m stems, and keeps doing it throughout the warm weather if cut back regularly. Plant *Leonotis* in a warm, sunny, well-drained position, and do not overwater. It is fairly drought resistant except in very hot weather. Prolonged frosts may damage growing tips, but as a rule the plant will recover quickly with the advent of warmer days, and is hardy down to −2°C/29°F. Grow from seed, divisions or semi-hardwood tip-cuttings taken in winter.

LEONOTIS leonurus
Lion's Ear

LEONOTIS 'Albiflora'
White Lion's Ear

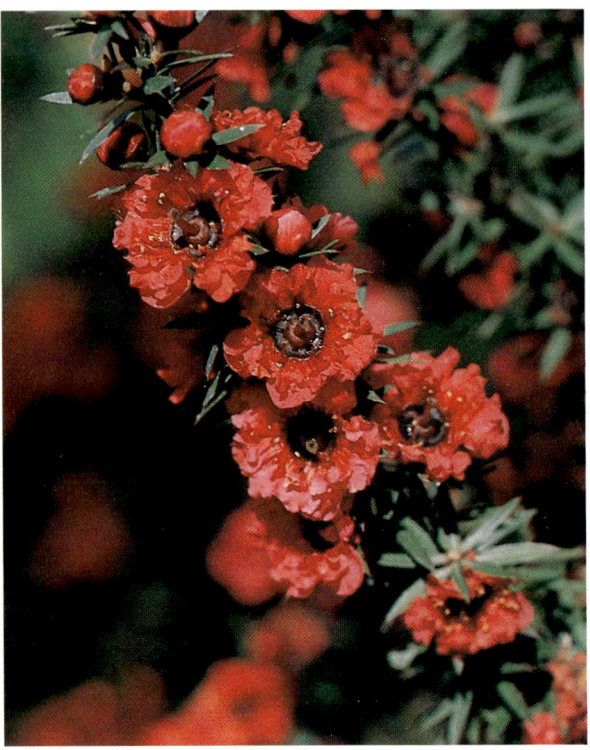

LEPTOSPERMUM 'Pacific Beauty'
Tea Tree

LEPTOSPERMUM

Tea Tree,
Manuka

☼ T

WINTER–SUMMER
AVERAGE/LONG DISPLAY
HT: 50-300cm/18-120in/SPREADING

Since Captain James Cook brewed a beverage from the tiny leaves of a *Leptospermum* the whole genus has been blessed with the name of Tea Tree. Between 30 and 40 species are recognized, all of them native to Australia and New Zealand. *Leptospermums* are by now deservedly popular shrubs all over the temperate world, for their graceful habit and soft, casual appearance make them ideal subjects for the informal landscape garden. Grown in full sun, they resist drought, wind and even salt spray. In fact the larger forms thrive on coastal cliffs or in sand dunes, where they assume a horizontal, contorted shape. In spring, all make a profuse display of small white, pink or red flowers, quite like peach blossom. Propagate from half-ripe cuttings, struck in summer in a sandy mix. No pruning is necessary.

LEPTOSPERMUM 'Red Damask'
Manuka

LEUCADENDRON

Gold Tips

☼ T

SUMMER
AVERAGE/LONG DISPLAY
HT: 1.8-7m/5-20ft

Relatively uncommon outside their native South
Africa, that country's 70-odd species of *Leucadendron* are remarkably decorative shrubs, but suffer by
comparison with their more floriferous cousins the
Proteas. In Protea, the flower is all important: in the
case of *Leucadendron* the foliage is decorative as
well—stiff, upward-pointing leaves that may be
smooth or silky, and are sometimes coloured silver,
gold or pink as well as green. They demand an acid,
well-drained soil, a sunny hillside position with
plenty of leaf-mould or peat, but not animal manure. Humidity keeps the plants thriving—even
ocean breezes. The actual flowers are not spectacular, colour is confined to the bracts (modified
leaves) that surround them. Difficult to propagate,
even from cuttings.

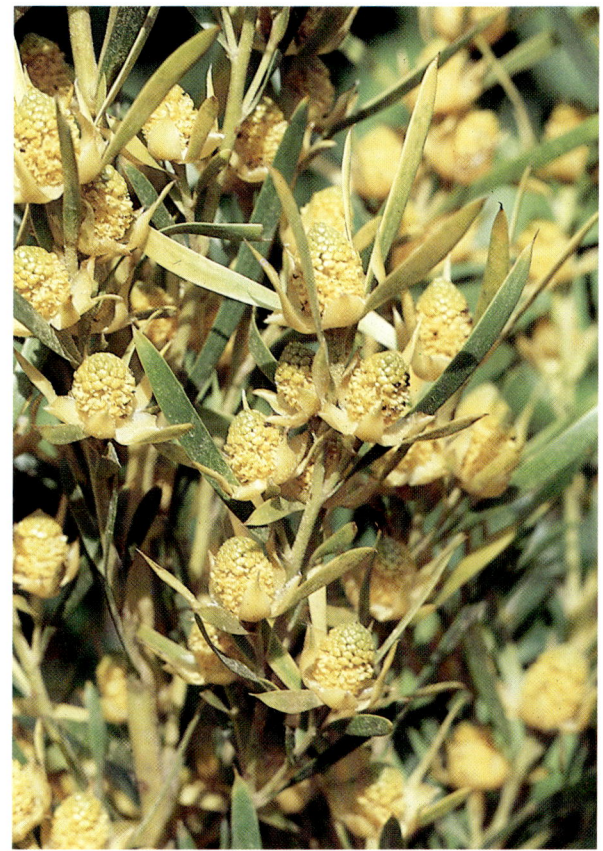

LEUCADENDRON salignum
Gold Tips

LEUCOSPERMUM

Pincushion

☼ T

WINTER–SUMMER
FAST/LONG DISPLAY
HT: 1-4m/3-13ft/SPREADING

Not the easiest of plants to get started, many of
South Africa's 30-odd species of *Leucospermum* have
been raised successfully in the western United
States, Australia and many other garden-oriented
parts of the world. Like the previous entry, they
enjoy a soil that is light and fast-draining, enriched
with leaf-mould but not animal manure. Regular
watering is a must, especially when young, and they
are propagated either from seed (which is erratic in
germination) or from cuttings struck with misting.
The foliage is generally smaller than that of related
Proteas and Leucadendrons, presenting a silver furry
appearance. *Leucospermums* quite enjoy a light frost,
and should be planted out small. They resent root
disturbance. Don't water directly onto the foliage.

LEUCOSPERMUM reflexum
Rocket Pincushion

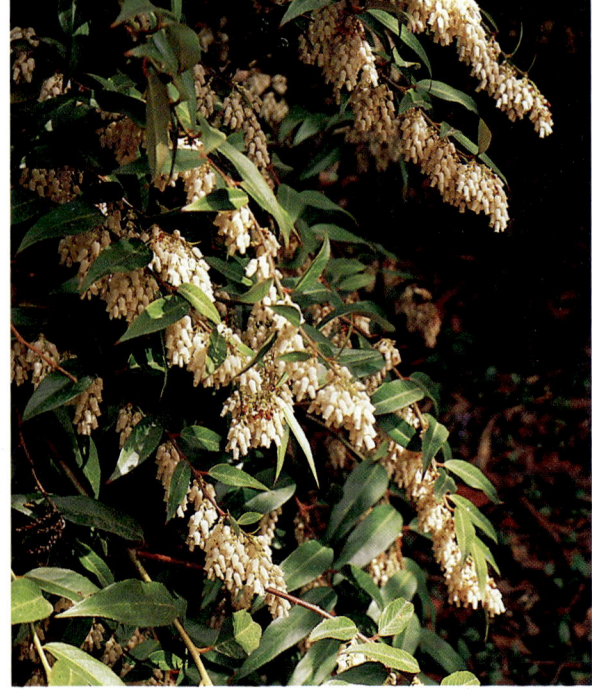

LEUCOSPERMUM tottum
Firewheel Pincushion

LEUCOTHOË
(syn ANDROMEDA) FRAGRANT

Dog Hobble,
Fetter Bush

☼
C T

SPRING
SLOW/LONG DISPLAY
HT: 2m/7ft/ARCHING

Named for one of the God Apollo's many lady-friends, the decorative genus *Leucothoë* includes some 50 decorative woodland plants, mostly from North America, but with others native to Asia, Malagasy and South America as well. Most are evergreen, with strongly reflexed leaves and showy racemes of lily-of-the-valley type flowers suspending from arching stems. These look sensational in large arrangements. Grow them from semi-hardwood tip-cuttings taken in late spring and struck over heat. They like a moist, acid soil and regular summer water. Hardy down to −8°C/18°F, even the ever-green types colour well in autumn.

LEUCOTHOË fontanesiana
Dog Hobble

LEYCESTERIA

Himalaya Honeysuckle

☼ ☀
C T

SUMMER–AUTUMN
FAST/LONG DISPLAY
HT: 2-3m/7-10ft/ERECT GROWTH

A small genus of Himalayan shrubs, the *Leycesterias* are closely related to the more common Honeysuckles (Lonicera spp.) and, like them, mostly deciduous. They enjoy a moderately rich, well-drained soil with high humidity, and are hardy down to −5°C/23°F in a sheltered position. In appropriately woodsy places, they send up closely-packed, arching stems, rather like bamboo, but decked with hanging spikes of claret-bracted white flowers. These are lightly fragrant, and followed by purplish, many-seeded fruits that are attractive to birds. The lightly-toothed leaves are covered with fine hair when young, colour well in autumn. They should be propagated from 20cm hardwood cuttings which are grown on for 12 months before autumn planting. Cut back flowered canes in early spring.

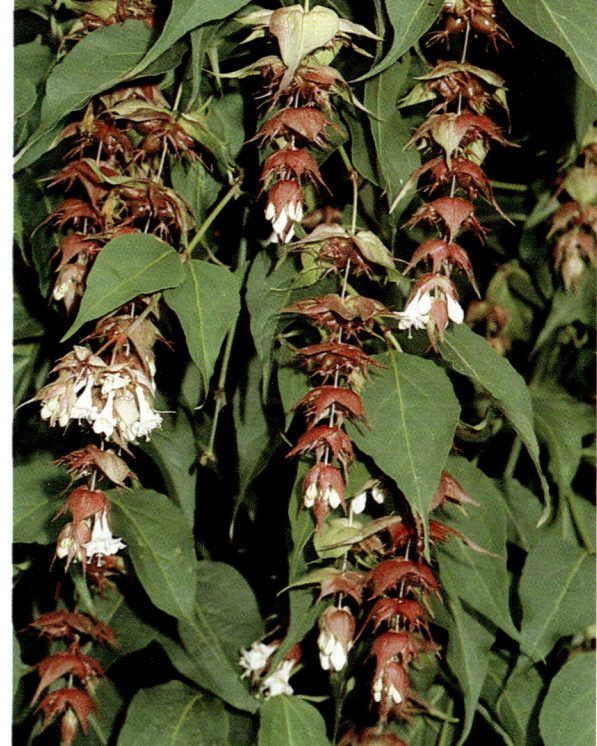

LEYCESTERIA formosa
Himalaya Honeysuckle

LITHODORA
(*syn* LITHOSPERMUM)

Heavenly Blue,
Puccoon

☼ ☀
T

SPRING–SUMMER
SLOW/LONG DISPLAY
HT: 10-30cm/4-12in/GROUND COVER

There's no more intense blue in nature than that found in the flowers of many *Lithodora* species, though there are white and yellow varieties of these attractive rockery plants as well. Some are perennials, some sub-shrubs, some true shrubs. Most prefer alkaline soil, but the illustrated *L. diffusa* or Heavenly Blue can't abide lime in any form. In cool, temperate mountain gardens it makes a stunning ground or rock cover in contrast with white Arabis and golden Aurinia, seeming to reflect the intense blue of mountain skies for months. It prefers full sun, except in hot areas, demands a well-drained soil and light watering even in summer. Grow from cuttings of last year's growth struck in a shaded mix of peat and sand. Shear after bloom.

LITHODORA diffusa
Heavenly Blue

LOROPETALUM 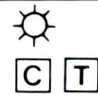 FRAGRANT

Fringe Flower,
Strap Flower

☼
C T

SPRING
FAST/LONG DISPLAY
HT: 60-300cm/2-10ft/SPREADING

Don't believe all the things you read about *Loro-petalum!* I was so used to hearing it described as a 'dwarf shrub for rockeries' that I was almost shocked to see it growing to 7m in Japan. Now we understand each other, and it looks most elegant in my garden as a series of dark, woody trunks topped with horizontal clouds of dainty foliage. The plant has downy twigs and leaves, and in spring, produces masses of fragrant cream flowers with strap-like petals. These resemble the flowers of Hamamelis, to which it is related. Grow from semi-hardwood cuttings taken in winter or summer and struck with bottom heat. Grow in a moderately rich soil, and keep the roots moist. Hardy down to −3°C/27°C. Shear lightly after bloom.

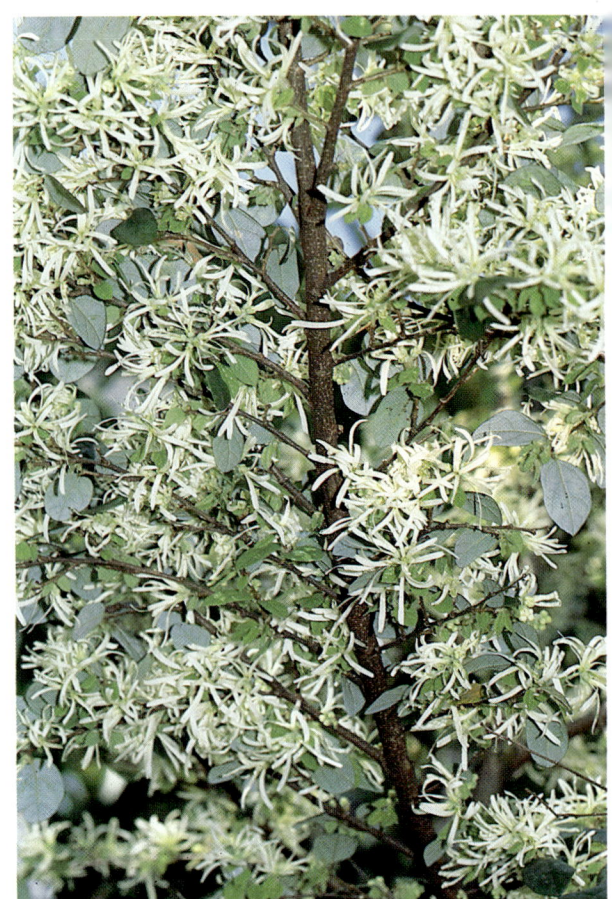

LOROPETALUM chinense
Fringe Flower

LUCULIA VERY FRAGRANT

(no popular name)

☼ T

AUTUMN–WINTER
AVERAGE/LONG DISPLAY
HT: 3-4m/10-13ft/IRREGULAR GROWTH

Most desirable and infuriating of autumn-flowering shrubs, the Himalayan beauty we call *Luculia* (from its native name *Luculi Swa*) has broken many gardeners' hearts. Just why does it die out so suddenly? Every expert has his own opinion! It adores warmth and humidity, but likes its roots to be cool at all times and left undisturbed. The colder the winter, the drier it should stay. It may be hardy down to −2°C/29°F, but should be protected from frost with a root cover of deep organic mulch. *Luculia gratissima* (one of 3 species) can be grown from seed or tip-cuttings struck spring or summer in individual pots. Cut it back heavily after bloom, and tip-prune to shape except when flower buds are forming. One of the most fragrant of all flowers, it can be grown under glass in colder climates.

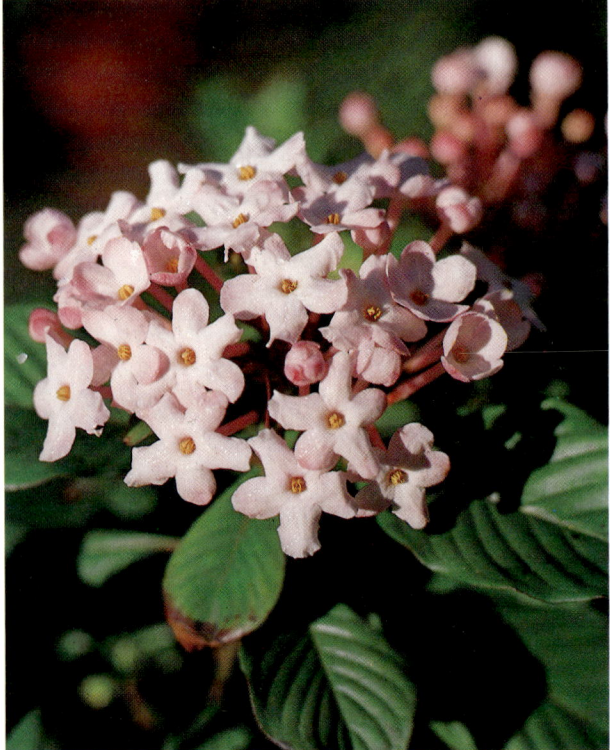

LUCULIA gratissima

MAHONIA

Oregon Grape

WINTER–SPRING
AVERAGE/LONG DISPLAY
HT: 1-4m/3-13ft/SPREADING

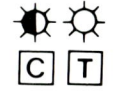

Shiny-clean shrubs with spiky holly-like leaves and plumes of golden blossom in spring or even earlier, the *Mahonias* are useful plants for hard conditions. Frosty or hot, shaded or dry, any position seems to suit them, and the flowers are usually followed by blue-black berries that look like grapes and often make a good jelly. Grow them in full sun in cool mountain places, in semi-shade where the temperatures are higher. They enjoy a rich, well-drained soil where they can sucker to their heart's content. Most easily propagated from rooted divisions, they can also be propagated from firm winter or autumn cuttings struck in a cool, moist place. Hardy down to at least −10°C/14°F, *Mahonias* can be rejuvenated by cutting spindly shoots right back. All species are from China or North America.

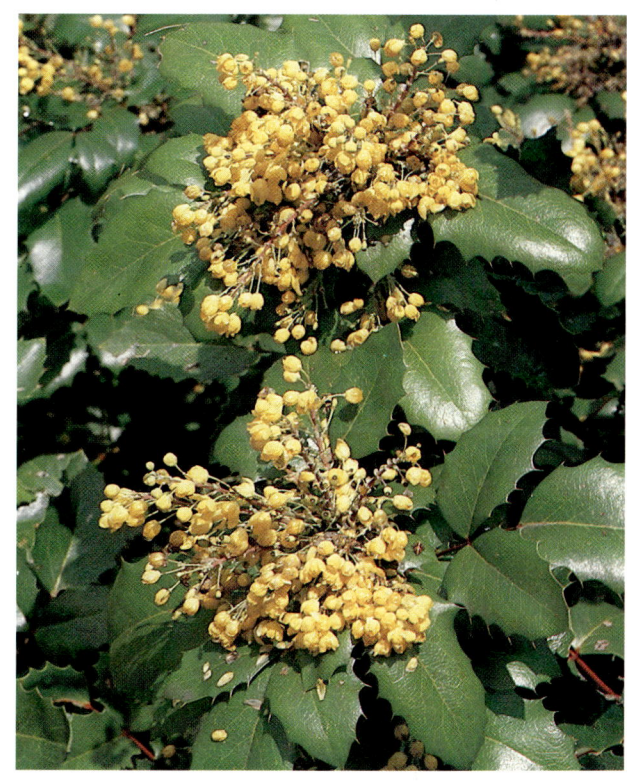

MAHONIA aquifolium
Oregon Grape

MAHONIA lomariifolia
Fern-leaf Mahonia

MALPIGHIA

Singapore Holly

SUMMER
SLOW/LONG DISPLAY
HT: 1-1.8m/3-6ft/SUCKERING

☼ ☀
T H

Not a holly, nor from Singapore either, this fine
example of botanical misnaming is a very worthwhile plant for the warm climate garden, where it
can be clipped into shape as a neat hedge or low
mound. The leaves are small, sharp and spiny, the
feathery flowers white to pink with a blur of golden
stamens, and sometimes there are tiny red fruits to
follow. *Malpighia coccigera* (one of about 30 species)
prefers a well-drained, moderately rich soil that is
kept continuously moist. With regular feeding it will
spread into a mass of cane-like trunklets. These
should be pruned to different heights if a good
foliage cover is desired. Propagate from cuttings of
almost-ripe shoots struck over heat.

MALPIGHIA coccigera
Singapore Holly

MALVAVISCUS
(*syn ACHANIA*)

Turk's Cap,
Cardinal's Hat,
Wax Mallow

☼
T H

SUMMER–WINTER
FAST/ALL SEASON
HT: 2-3m/7-10ft

If your scarlet-flowered Hibiscus fails to open, but
produces many vivid hanging buds, it is probably not
a Hibiscus at all, but the related *Malvaviscus* or
Turk's Cap, a showy South American plant which
blooms all through the warmer weather in subtropical climates. It is particularly stunning where
the humidity stays high and the sun is lightly
filtered. Propagate from semi-hardwood cuttings
struck in winter or early spring in a warm, moist
place, or layer from naturally low-growing branches.
Enriched, light sandy soil is best, so long as it can be
kept well drained, but *Malvaviscus* can also be raised
in large containers. The leaves are ovate, toothed,
about 20cm in length. Flowers are generally scarlet,
but there is a pale pink variety.

MALVAVISCUS mollis
Turk's Cap

MEDINILLA

Javanese Rhododendron

SUMMER
SLOW/LONG DISPLAY
HT: 50-250cm/1½-8ft/PENDULOUS

Unless you live in the tropics, or can afford to run a heated conservatory, you're not likely to enjoy the showy blooms of this most gorgeous of tropical plants. For *Medinillas* are fussy growers, and even in winter demand a night temperature of at least 21°C/70°F if they're to do at all well. And as anyone with a recent central heating bill can testify, winter temperatures like that don't come cheap. There are some 100 species of these remarkable shrubs, mostly native to South-east Asia and certain of the Pacific

Islands, but the only one much seen away from its native islands is M. *magnifica*, sometimes called the Javanese Rhododendron, though in fact it comes from the Philippines. It is propagated from cuttings of half-ripened wood in spring. These are potted up in a mixture of sifted peat, sand and fine charcoal, and kept in a humid glasshouse until they strike. *Medinillas* may be kept permanently in containers of moderate size, but must be repotted regularly to freshen up the soil. Fertilize from time to time, prune to shape after bloom and syringe with dilute miticide in water to discourage the attentions of red spider mite, particularly on the reverse sides of all leaves. The fantastic pendant flower-clusters appear in late spring. They combine strawberry pink flowers and mauve-pink bracts with purple and yellow stamens.

MEDINILLA magnifica
Javanese Rhododendron

MEGASKEPASMA

Brazilian Red-cloak,
Megas

☼ ◐
T H

AUTUMN
FAST/LONG DISPLAY
HT: 3m/10ft

A spectacular shrub for mass display in the *very* warm climate garden, tongue-twisting *Megaskepasma erthrochlamys* (gasp!) is sometimes known as Brazilian Red-cloak, though in fact it comes from Venezuela. It is a member of the acanthus family and bears more than a passing resemblance to Aphelandra, Jacobinia, Pachystachys and Sanchezia, all popular house plants in recent years. It is not cold hardy, but if you live in a warm enough climate it is easy to propagate from cuttings. Growing plants enjoy a light, leaf-rich soil with regular water and fertilizer, and look best in semi-shade, which reduces the transpiration from their large leaf areas. The showy panicles of crimson bloom appear in autumn.

MEGASKEPASMA erythrochlamys
Brazilian Red-cloak

MELALEUCA   FRAGRANT

Honeymyrtle,
Bottlebrush,
Paperbark

☼ T

SPRING–SUMMER
FAST/LONG DISPLAY
HT: 1.5-6m/5-20ft

To all intents and purposes exclusively Australian (though some species are found on islands further north), *Melaleucas* are particularly noted for their showy blossoms and decorative, peeling bark. Most species are evergreen and provide a dense foliage cover or windbreak. They make do with only occasional watering in dry times, need little or no fertilizing and are not at all particular as to soil provided the drainage is reasonable. Even poor, sandy soil will produce a good display of the curious compound flower spikes. *Melaleucas* are known collectively as Paperbarks, Bottlebrushes or Honeymyrtles, though the first name belongs more appropriately to the tree species which produce great, spongey sheets of readily peeling bark that can be

MELALEUCA lateritia
Robin Redbreast Bush

used for fencing, roofing or lining hanging baskets. Bottlebrush does describe the flower forms of many species, but also serves to confuse them even further with the related Callistemons (which see earlier in this book). Honeymyrtle seems entirely appropriate as a popular generic name. *Melaleuca* (the botanical name means 'black and white', describing the contrast between the dark, often needle-like foliage and white, papery bark) can be grown from seed, sown in spring in a light, peaty mix with scant cover, or from 5cm semi-hardwood cuttings struck over heat from summer to midwinter. The illustrated species have a sweet, honey scent, aromatic foliage and attract birds from far and wide. They grow well by the coast, even in salt sea air, where they often adopt picturesque shapes. But probably their most popular use is sheared to a compact shape and used as a windbreak. In this form their profusion of bloom is greatly stimulated.

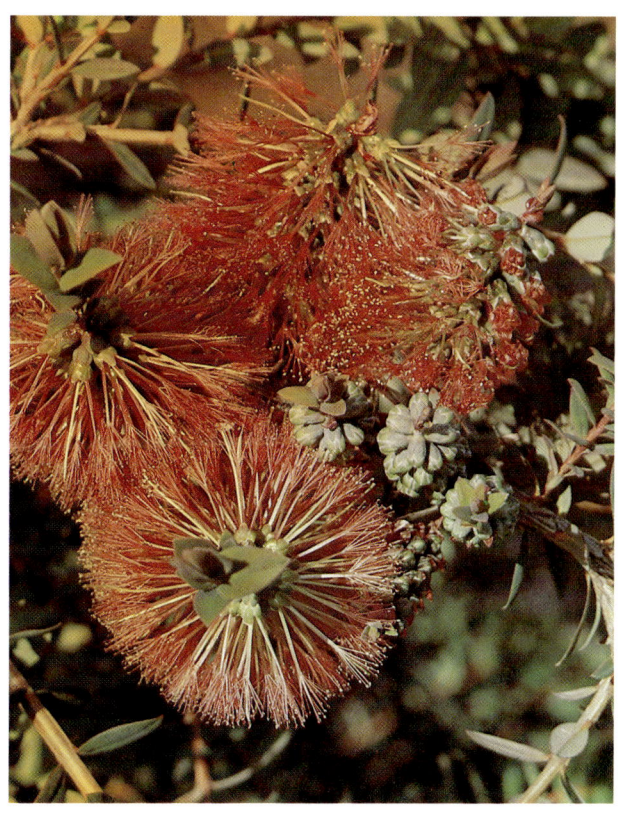

MELALEUCA *hypericifolia*
Red-flowered Honeymyrtle

MELALEUCA *armillaris*
Bracelet Honeymyrtle

MELASTOMA

Pink Lasiandra,
Blue Tongue

T H

SUMMER–AUTUMN
FAST/LONG DISPLAY IN HOT CLIMATE
HT: TO 2m/6ft

Found in most tropic areas except the Americas, the 40-odd species of *Melastoma* greatly resemble the related *Tibouchinas* (which see) and have a flowering season centring on summer in temperate climates. From this, the hotter it gets, the longer period they bloom. The leaves are typically spear-shaped and leathery, with strongly delineated parallel veins. Open 5-petalled flowers cluster at the ends of branches, and may be pink, purple or (rarely) white. They are followed by edible blue-black berries that stain the mouth and tongue, and have led to one of the plant's popular names. Propagate all species from semi-hardwood cuttings struck in late winter under warm, humid conditions. Prune lightly to shape. *Melastomas* are not really cold hardy.

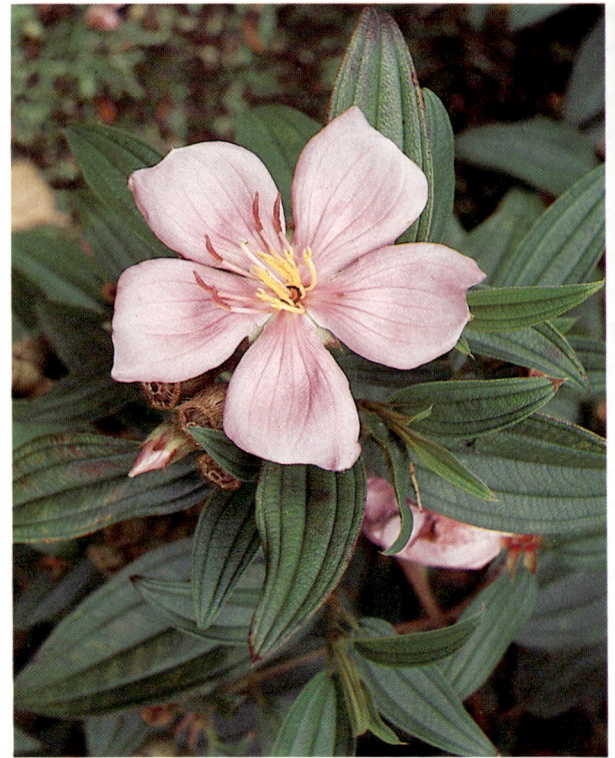

MELASTOMA polyanthum
Blue Tongue

MENZIESIA

Mock Azalea,
Minniebush

C T

SPRING–SUMMER
SLOW/LONG DISPLAY
HT: 40-70cm/1½-2½ft

Found naturally in both Japan and North America, the half-dozen or so species of *Menziesia* are delightful small shrubs for the shaded, woodsy, lime-free garden. They are deciduous, and perhaps when not in bloom could be mistaken for small Azaleas. But when the terminal flower clusters open in spring, the likeness disappears immediately. For the blooms are distinctly bell or urn shaped. Easily propagated from winter-sown seed, layers or 7cm cuttings taken with a heel in summer, these woodland charmers have only two needs: a humid atmosphere and perfect drainage. They are almost completely cold hardy and not much affected by frost, at least when planted under trees. Keep their roots continuously moist in warm weather, and shop around for flower colours which include pink, red, cream and greenish-white according to species.

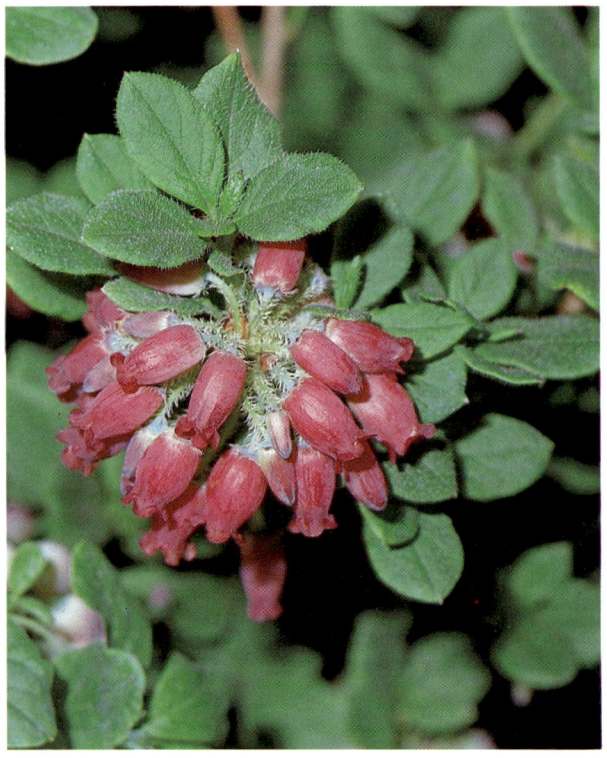

MENZIESIA ciliicalyx
Mock Azalea

MICHELIA

Portwine Magnolia,
Banana Shrub

☼ [T]

SPRING
SLOW/SCANT DISPLAY
HT: 2-6m/6-20ft/DENSELY FOLIAGED

There's a mystery at the bottom of our gardens, masquerading under the name *Michelia figo*! Northern hemisphere books call it Banana Shrub, say it has small, flat creamy-yellow flowers smelling like ripe bananas. True! But in the southern hemisphere we call it the Portwine Magnolia. Its small flowers never open fully, are the colour of a rich port wine. And it *does* smell like port wine, not bananas! I believe they are two different species, and that botanists have for once become confused in the matter of synonymy. *Michelia fuscata* and M. *figo*—but which is which?

Grow either from semi-hardwood cuttings taken in summer and autumn. Prune lightly all over after bloom to keep the plant dense and compact.

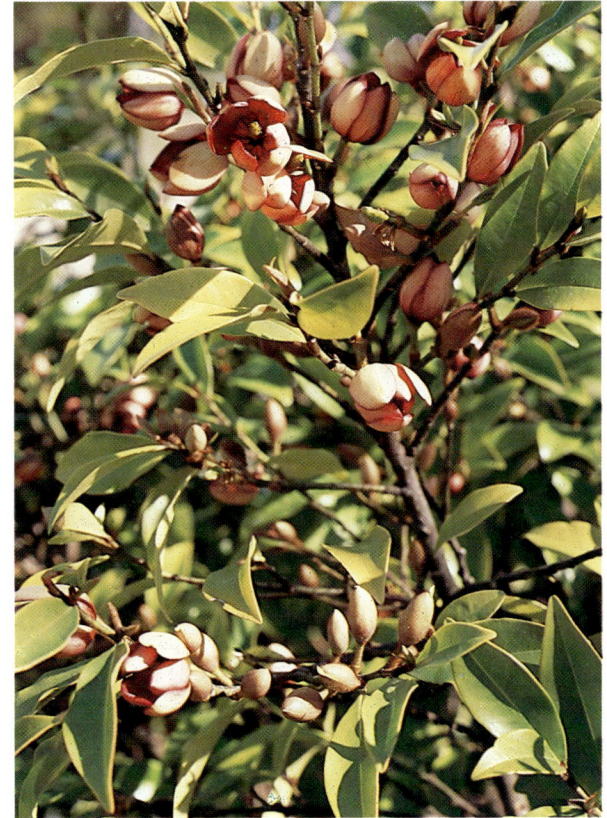

MICHELIA figo
Portwine Magnolia

MIMETES
(syn *OROTHAMNUS*)

South African Bottlebrush,
Soldaat

☼
[C] [T]

WINTER–SPRING
SLOW/LONG DISPLAY
HT: TO 1.25m/4ft/ROUNDED

One of the rarest of the Proteaceae in cultivation: *Mimetes* is seldom seen outside South Africa. The 16 species have stem-clasping leathery leaves overlapping like fish-scales. Those towards branch tips colour a rosy pink in season, and part slightly to reveal a mass of red or pink-tipped stamens partly protected by a colourful bract. Illustrated M. *argentea* or Silver-leaf Bottlebrush is covered with silvery hairs in all its parts. Like other *Mimetes* it needs an acid soil, enriched with vegetable compost, but not animal manure. Drainage should be fast, but the soil must never dry out. These beautiful plants enjoy a warm, humid climate, but have been known to withstand 15 degrees of frost.

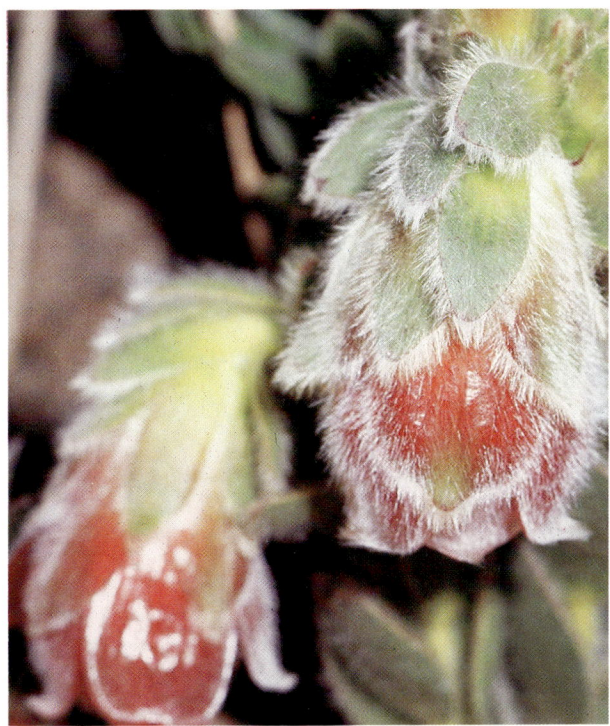

MIMETES argentea
Silverleaf Bottlebrush

MIMULUS
(syn DIPLACUS)

Monkeyflower

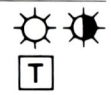

SPRING–SUMMER
FAST/LONG DISPLAY
HT: TO 1.5m/5ft

Far and away the majority of *Mimulus* species seen in gardens of the world are perennial or annual. But North America, particularly in its western states, is home to a number of shrubby species, formerly classed as Diplacus. These include *M. aridus*, *M. aurantiacus*, *M. longiflorus* and the illustrated *M. puniceus*. This is a many-branched shrub growing to 1.5m and with a clammy, even sticky feel to all its parts. It is grown from seed (which should be scarcely covered by sand), from cuttings, or from rooted divisions of the entire plant. The shrubby *Mimulus* species like a well-drained soil, regular water even in the colder weather. Its brittle stems will probably need to be cut right back to the ground and mulched in frosty areas. The 8cm leaves are narrow, the single flowers a coppery red.

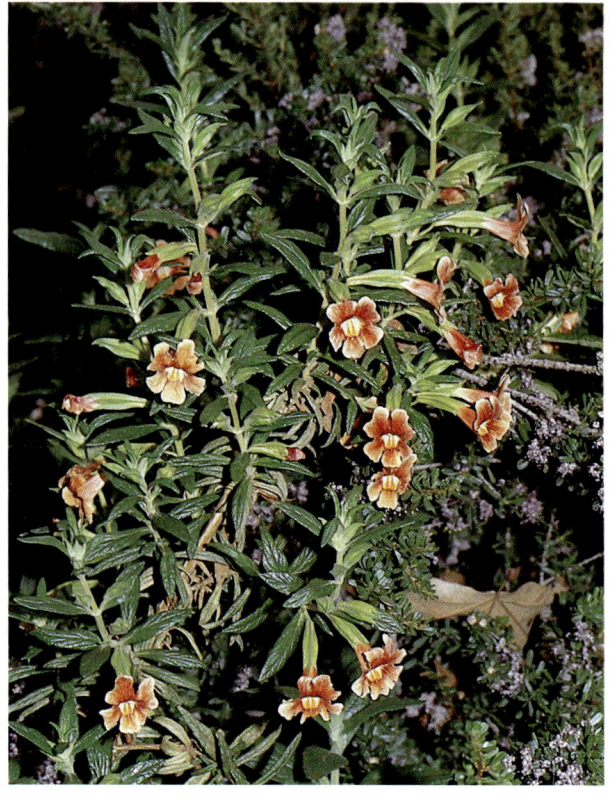

MIMULUS puniceus
Bush Monkeyflower

MONTANOA

Tree Daisy,
Daisy Tree

AUTUMN–WINTER
FAST/LONG DISPLAY
HT: TO 6m/20ft

Growing naturally throughout Central America is a large and spectacular genus of daisies, some of which must reach to 6m in height in a warm climate. They make truly sensational background plants in the subtropical garden, where their year-round display of deeply-divided leaves is joined in late winter by long, branching stems of gold centred, snowy daisy flowers. Don't even attempt them in cold winter areas though, for the brittle, pithy stems collapse at the first touch of frost. *Montanoa* species can be grown from seed and from stem or root cuttings struck with heat. Being such large plants, they need a heavy, well-enriched soil and plenty of water. Deadhead regularly to maintain appearance.

MONTANOA hibiscifolia
Daisy Tree

MURRAYA

Mock Orange,
Cosmetic Bark,
Orange Jessamine

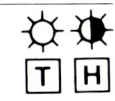

SPRING–AUTUMN
FAST/REPEATED DISPLAY
HT: TO 3m/10ft/DENSE FOLIAGE

Jasmine fragrance and clustered flowers like orange blossom earn *Murraya* a place in any warm-climate garden. And as if all that floral beauty were not enough in any one year, *Murraya* will repeat the display several times over the warmer months, following each blooming with a sprinkling of orange-scarlet fruits like tiny citrus. Full sun brings on the best flowering, except in really hot climates where semi-shade will protect the glossy, evergreen foliage. *Murraya paniculata* (syn M. *exotica*) likes a well-drained soil rich in leaf-mould and constant summer water. It should be sheared after the last autumn blooming to encourage heavy flowering the following season, and suffers badly in cold winters. From India and Malaysia, *Murraya* is easily struck over heat from heeled cuttings taken in winter.

MURRAYA *paniculata*
Orange Jessamine

MUSSAENDA

Buddha's Lamp,
Flag Bush,
Ashanti Blood

SUMMER–AUTUMN (WINTER IN TROPICS)
FAST/LONG DISPLAY
HT: 2-3m/6-10ft/SPREADING

These curious tropical shrubs put on a brilliant display in warm climates—though on close inspection, the colour is supplied largely by occasional oversized sepals, the flowers being quite uninteresting. *Mussaendas* are of particular interest in the Philippines (to which several species are native) because of a series of beautiful cultivars named for the wives of regional rulers, e.g. 'Queen Sirikit', 'Gining Imelda'. In the right climate, all species can be propagated from thin hardwood cuttings taken in midwinter and kept both warm and humid. A light fibrous soil is best, with ample summer water. Prune heavily after bloom to force further flowers. African *M. erythrophylla* is quite drought resistant in mild winter areas.

MUSSAENDA *erythrophylla*
Ashanti Blood

MUSSAENDA philippica
Buddha's Lamp

MUSSAENDA 'Gining Imelda'
Flag Bush

NERIUM

Oleander,
Rose Bay

☼ T H

LATE SPRING–AUTUMN
FAST/LONG DISPLAY
HT: 1-4m/3-12ft

Most useful of shrubs wherever the climate is warm enough (above −5°C/23°F), the Mediterranean's sturdy Oleanders (*Nerium oleander*) are astonishingly resistant to neglect, and thrive in the toughest of conditions, blooming away for months even in the most polluted of industrial areas, where they are often used for street plantings. They are the perfect choice in seaside gardens where they seem unworried by salt air; equally spectacular in dry, semi-desert places or soils with poor drainage and heavy salinity. In normal garden conditions they are unmatched in the profusion of their bloom. Olean-

ders are somewhat bulky plants, sending up many erect suckers. But with regular pruning they can be trained to single-trunked shape, or forced into an almost 2-dimensional hedge. All parts of Oleander are poisonous, however, and they are best not planted where stock might be tempted to feed on them. The dark, glossy, evergreen leaves are spear-shaped and 10 to 15cm long; the flowers, 5-7.5cm in diameter, are clustered densely at branch ends and come in a variety of colours—white, pink, apricot, red and pale yellow. They may be single or double, and improve in both size and colour as the weather warms up. All colour varieties are easily propagated from 8-10cm semi-hardwood cuttings taken in autumn and set in containers of standard sand/peat mixture with warmth and humidity. They may even be rooted in jars of plain water. Heavy pruning of old flowered wood is done in early spring—unwanted suckers should be pulled, not cut away. Watch and spray for aphids.

NERIUM oleander 'Algiers'

NERIUM 'Sister Agnes'

NERIUM 'Dr Golfin'

NERIUM 'Punctatum'

NERIUM 'Yellow'

OCHNA

Carnival Bush,
Mickey Mouse Plant,
Bird's Eye Plant

SPRING–SUMMER
FAST/LONG SEASON
HT: 1-2m/3-7ft/SPREADING

No worries about propagating this one—any friend who has an *Ochna* bush will soon find seedlings everywhere, though that is only likely to happen in a warm climate. The common species is *O. serrulata* from South Africa, but other species are quite similar. All can be grown from fresh seed, or from cuttings of half-ripened wood taken in summer or autumn. *Ochna* will grow in almost any soil so long as it is well-drained, but a slightly acid pH is preferred. It positively thrives in seaside salt air with regular water. Bronzy new spring foliage is followed by yellow buttercup flowers which soon fall, leaving the sepals to turn a bright scarlet. Within these appear shining black berries. Prune after fruit-fall to induce a more compact growth. A good hedge plant.

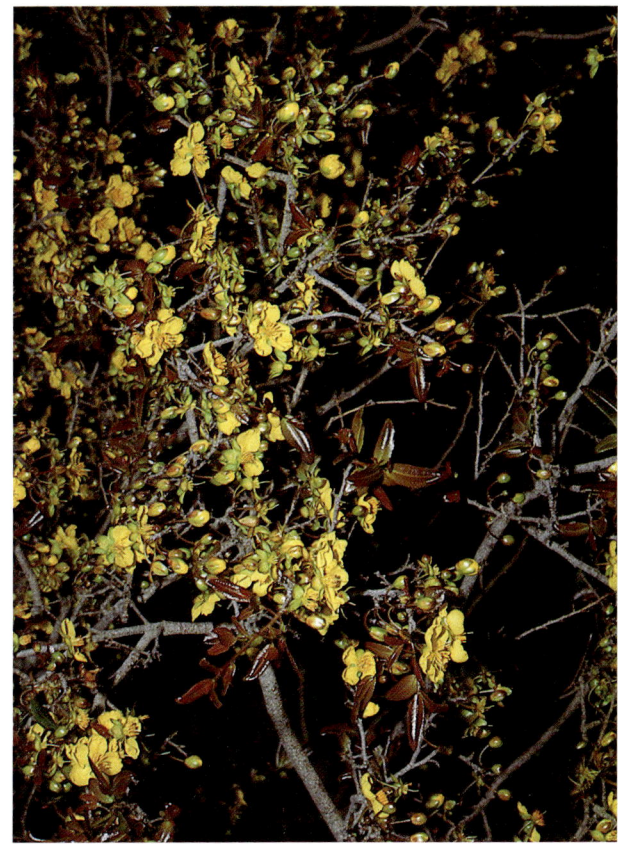

OCHNA serrulata
Mickey Mouse Plant

ODONTONEMA
(syn *THYRSACANTHUS, JUSTICIA*)

Red Justicia

SUMMER–AUTUMN
FAST/LONG DISPLAY
HT: TO 1.5m/5ft/ERECT

Outside the true tropics, a warm patio or sheltered sunny aspect is necessary to bring out the best in *Odontonemas*, for they need constant warmth and moisture and protection from winds which so easily snap the brittle stems. Even so, *O. strictum* is the only one of 30 species you are likely to see. Its shiny, elliptic leaves are borne in opposite pairs all the way up tall, dark stems. The warm weather flower display is spectacular, but useless for cutting, as the narrow, tubular flowers open irregularly and drop all over the place. *Odontonemas* enjoy a moderately rich soil with good drainage, and can be grown from soft tip-cuttings struck at any time through the warmer months. Tip-prune and deadhead regularly to promote bushiness, cut back hard in winter.

ODONTONEMA strictum
Red Justicia

OLEARIA
(syn EURYBIA)

Daisybush,
Tree Aster

SPRING–SUMMER
AVERAGE/LONG DISPLAY
HT: 1.5m/5ft/COMPACT

Scarcely to be numbered among the more spectacular plants of the Australian area, the *Olearias* or Daisybushes have won a northern hemisphere following out of all proportion to their beauty. True, they mostly hail from cooler parts of Australia and New Zealand and might be expected to be climatically suited to England, but they seem too frost-tender even there.

Their foliage is evergreen, their blooming profuse until late in the season. They enjoy a well-drained loam in full sun and are quite useful in seaside gardens. Of over a hundred and more species, the majority have white daisy flowers, with a few in washed-out mauve. Some have no petals around the centre dish at all. *Olearias* do better without cultivation around the roots.

OLEARIA *subrepanda*
Daisybush

OLEARIA *moschata*
Tree Aster

OSBECKIA
(syn LASIANDRA, MELASTOMA)

Rough-leaf Osbeckia

SPRING–AUTUMN
AVERAGE/LONG DISPLAY
HT: 1-1.5m/3-5ft/LOOSE SHAPE

These brilliantly coloured shrubs look so much like Lasiandras (see entry *Tibouchina*), one wonders why they have been given another name. And then, checking in my library, I see *Osbeckias* come from Asia and Africa, whereas the lookalike *Tibouchinas* are from tropical America. Still, a difference in origin is not usually sufficient reason to give a plant a different name, so there has to be more than meets the eye about these eye-catching flowers. They're easy to grow from soft tip-cuttings taken in spring. They prefer a light soil that is friable, and they're inclined to grow naturally sparse if you don't give them a light, all-over prune in late winter. Flowers are pink, purple or red, borne terminally. Some leaves will colour brilliantly in cold weather.

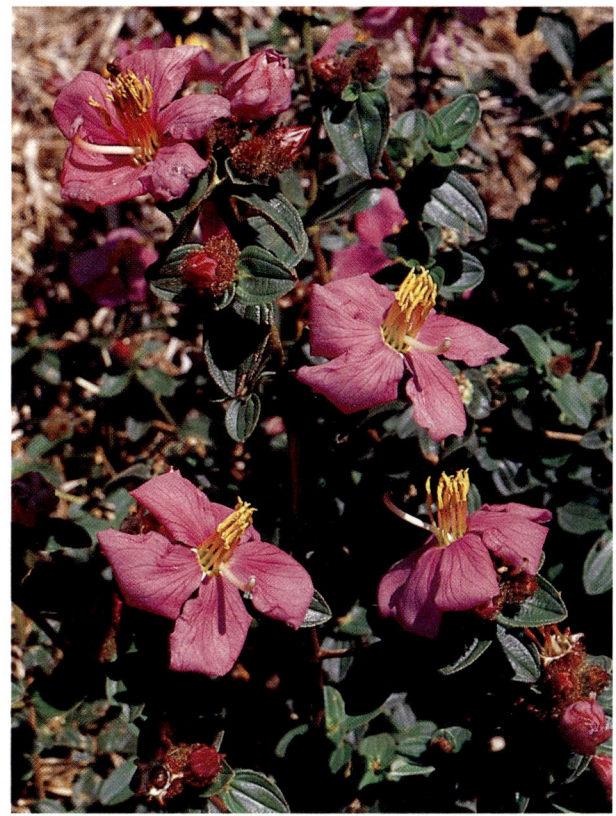

OSBECKIA X *kewensis*
Hybrid Osbeckia

OSMANTHUS   FRAGRANT

Fragrant Olive,
Kwai-fa

AUTUMN–SPRING
SLOW/LONG DISPLAY
HT: 2-4m/7-12ft/SPARSE

To many people, the most delicious fragrance of all is the unforgettable perfume of *Osmanthus fragrans*—a blend of Jasmine, Gardenia and ripe apricots. A rather sparse shrub with glossy, toothed leaves that almost hide the minute flowers (which are used in Chinese jasmine tea), it can be trained as a small tree, an espalier, even as a rough sort of hedge. I keep mine in a sunny sheltered spot outside the kitchen door where its fragrance is a joy from autumn right through to spring. *O. fragrans* is only one of 40 evergreen species, but far and away the best. Propagate it from leafy tip-cuttings set over heat during autumn and winter. The growing plants will enjoy a moderately rich, well-drained soil with plenty of water in dry weather. The tiny creamy flowers appear mostly at leaf axils.

OSMANTHUS *fragrans*
Kwai-fa

PAEONIA *suffruticosa*
'Yacryo Tsusaki'

PAEONIA *suffruticosa*
'Rock's Variety'

PAEONIA FRAGRANT

Moutan,
Tree Peony

☼ ☀
C

SPRING
SLOW/SHORT DISPLAY
HT: 1-2m/3-7ft

Two thousand years ago, the Chinese called these silken-flowered, perfumed beauties 'the king of flowers'—and king of flowers they still are to gardeners fortunate enough to live where the climate is right for them. They are not hard to grow, given the deep, rich soil they need, but a cold winter is the real key to success, for they originate in hard-winter areas of Tibet, western China, Siberia and Mongolia. They grow to perfection in mountainous areas of most English-speaking countries.

Basically, there are two types, the more common being perennials, often hybrids of *Paeonia lactiflora.* But the type we deal with here are the so-called Tree Peonies, a handful of species of sparse, woody, deciduous shrubs that grow to 2m tall. They are

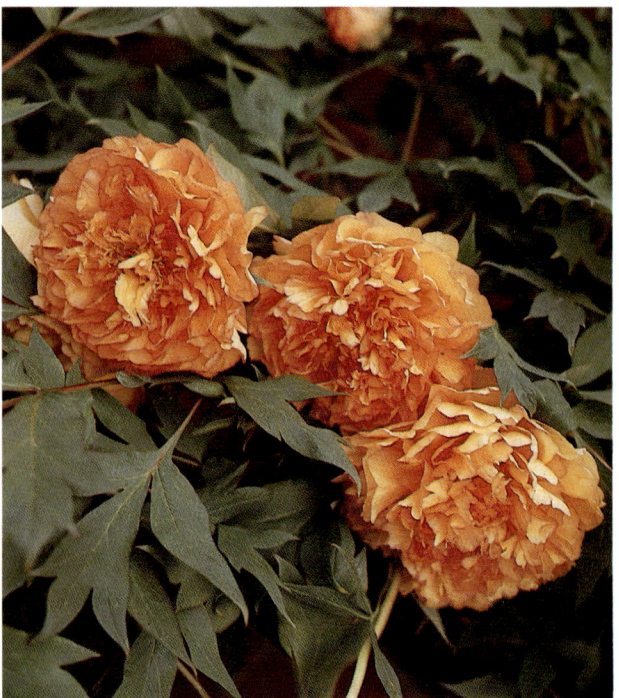

PAEONIA X *lutea*
'Souvenir de Maxim Cornu'

PAEONIA suffruticosa
'Suzakuman'

great favourites in larger, cool-climate gardens, and are best planted among other shrubs with protection from morning sun which damages the dew-wet blossoms. Tree Peonies of most species bear the larger flowers (up to 22cm in diameter) but have fewer petals than the perennial types. They also have a wider range of colours—every shade from darkest red to white, with some in tones of purple, orange and yellow.

Tree peonies are usually bought as grafted plants, but can be grown from 20cm hardwood cuttings taken in autumn. They are slow-growing plants, but long-lived. Little care is needed except to prune dead wood in spring.

Before planting, the soil should be dug at least spade deep, and liberally enriched with well-decayed manure and compost. Set the young plants out in mild weather during the colder months, with the grafting union about 7.5cm below the soil surface. Dress with bone meal, and mulch annually with well-rotted manure in spring; water liberally during dry weather and never, *never* disturb the plants once they're set in place. All species of Tree Peony can be raised from seed, which is produced liberally, but they won't come true to colour and will take up to three years to bloom. Peonies are relatively disease free.

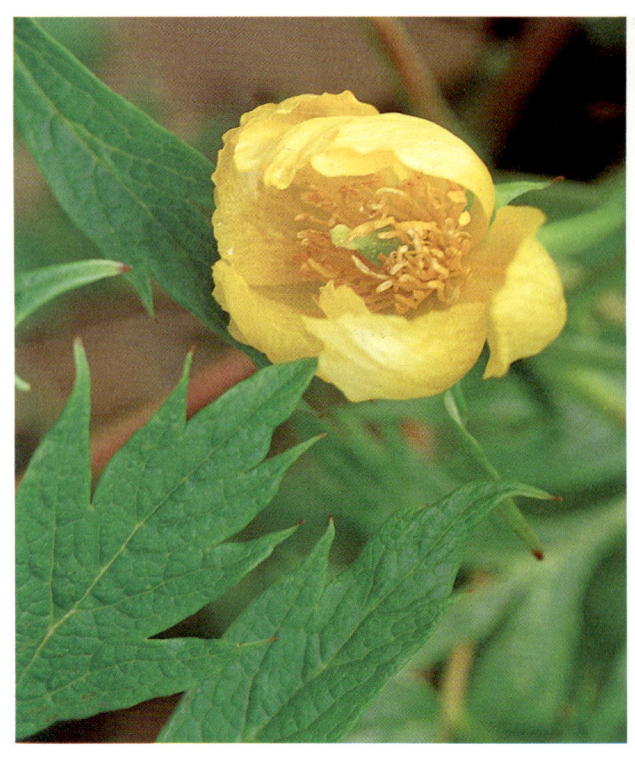

PAEONIA lutea
Golden Tree Peony

PAEONIA X *lemoinei*
'l'Esperance'

PENTAS

Egyptian Star Cluster

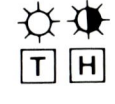

SPRING–AUTUMN
VERY FAST/ALL SEASON
HT: 60-100cm/2-3ft

A colourful genus of compact shrubs from tropical Africa, *Pentas* somewhat resemble Bouvardia, and are grown easily from soft tip-cuttings. These may be taken any time from spring to early autumn, and must be struck with warmth and humidity. In spite of its tropic origin, *Pentas* will grow in any frost-free climate, but prefers a wet summer and warm winter. Well-drained sandy soil is best, preferably rich with leaf-mould, and regular pinching back will encourage a neat, bushy habit. Be sure to deadhead regularly, and shorten flowered stems slightly in early spring. *Pentas* species are very much at home by the sea, in rock gardens or as a massed bedding plant. Illustrated *P. lanceolata* commonly blooms in a rosy-mauve shade, but has white and scarlet varieties. Its cultivar 'Coccinea' is a larger plant with brilliant carmine flowers and strongly ribbed leaves.

PENTAS lanceolata
Egyptian Star Cluster

PETROPHILE

Drumsticks,
Conesticks

SPRING
AVERAGE/LONG DISPLAY
HT: 50-200cm/20-80in/SPREADING

Yet another interesting genus of the Protea family, this time almost exclusively from Western Australia, the *Petrophiles* (ancient Greek for rock lovers) huddle in dry, perfectly drained, rocky places, and make up in texture what they lose in colour. Illustrated *P. linearis* both looks and feels like a mass of pink pipe cleaners. The leaves are thick, sickle-shaped and about 5cm in length. Stems are woody, and the flower clusters are followed by interesting fruits that have the texture of pine cones. *Petrophiles* are mostly grown from seed, which germinates in about 2 months. They grow best in a continuously warm sandy soil, and do not care for humidity at all. When you cut the flowers, pruning is unnecessary.

PETROPHILE linearis
Drumsticks

PHILADELPHUS FRAGRANT

Mock Orange,
Syringa

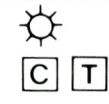

LATE SPRING–SUMMER
AVERAGE/SHORT DISPLAY
HT: 1-4m/3-13ft/FOUNTAIN SHAPE

The overpowering orange-blossom fragrance of *Philadelphus* should be reason enough for its presence in any summer garden plan. But when you add masses of golden-centred, snowy flowers on tall, arching canes, the effect is irresistible. Though all are similar, more than 40 separate species are recognized, hailing from all three continents of the northern hemisphere. They are easy shrubs to grow, will flourish in almost any soil—even turning on a good display where the pH is alkaline. Dependent on the height of individual species, they may be used in open borders, as wall shrubs, or along pathways, where the tall, arching canes will bring heads of bloom close to the passer-by. Individual plants should be thinned out after bloom, cutting away the oldest wood altogether. New plants strike from 6cm soft tip-cuttings or 15cm pieces of semi-hardwood in summer and autumn. They must be kept warm and humid until new roots are established.

PHILADELPHUS X 'Belle Etoile'
Blushing Mock Orange

PHILADELPHUS mexicanus
Mexican Mock Orange

Most species are deciduous, though *P. mexicanus* for one stays evergreen in warmer climates. Leaves vary from 5 to 9cm in length according to variety, except in the illustrated *P. microphyllus* where they rarely pass 2cm. In some species they are smooth above, hairy below; others reverse the pattern. All have a distinct crêpy texture. Flowers appear terminally, sometimes singly, sometimes in large clusters. They are snowy white, 4-petalled except in the CV 'Virginal' which generally presents a number of double blooms. Species *P. coulteri*, sometimes called the Rose Syringa, has petals stained with purple red. This effect is more commonly seen in its hybrid CV 'Belle Etoile'.

Very useful as they flower well after most other spring shrubs have finished, most *Philadelphus* species are both drought and cold resistant, though regular watering pays dividends in growth.

PHILADELPHUS coronarius
Common Mock Orange

PHILADELPHUS X 'Virginal'
Double Mock Orange

PHILADELPHUS microphyllus
Small-leaf Mock Orange

PHOTINIA

Japanese Photinia

SPRING
AVERAGE/LONG DISPLAY
HT: 1.5-3m/5-10ft/DENSE

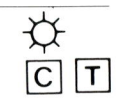

A popular bedding plant, especially in cooler areas, the Japanese Photinia (*Photinia glabra*) is most often seen in its two cultivars, 'Rubra' which has brilliant red new foliage, and 'Robusta' which has larger leaves of a somewhat bronzier red. In all types, the colourful spring foliage is followed by large flat panicles of tiny, acrid-smelling white flowers. These are followed by blue-black berries and finally, brilliant autumn colouring, for *Photinia* is semi-deciduous, losing a proportion of leaves each year. Foliage is shiny and brightly toothed, and the plants may be propagated from seed or semi-hardwood tip-cuttings taken with a heel during the colder months. *Photinias* are customarily pruned regularly to keep them dense, and are hardy down to −10°C/14°F.

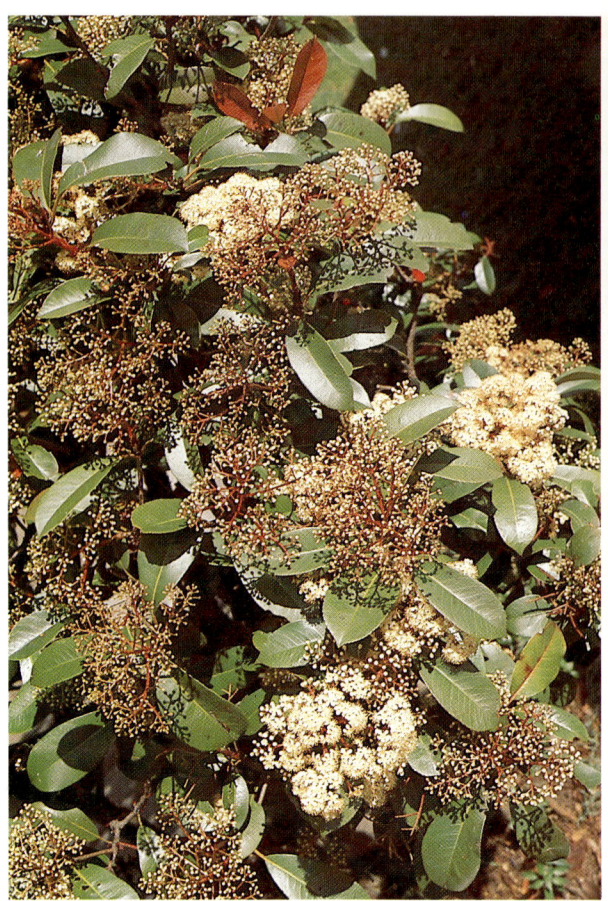

PHOTINIA glabra
Japanese Photinia

PHYLICA

Flannel Bush,
Featherhead

WINTER
AVERAGE/LONG DISPLAY
HT: TO 1.2m/4ft

Not a member of the Protea family (though from its appearance you might think so), the dainty Featherhead is a small, erect shrub rarely passing 1.2m in height. As in many of the South African flora, it is not the flowers that catch the eye, but the bracts surrounding them. The true flowers are inside these in a composite mass, and individually are about the size of a pin's head. *Phylicas* (there are almost 150 species of them) are evergreen, have downy new growth, narrow, heath-like leaves and thrive in salt air, close to the sea. They must have humidity and a well-drained acid soil. They may be propagated from seed or from autumn cuttings of half-ripened shoots. *Phylicas* cut well for long-lasting displays, and if sufficient are picked, need no further pruning.

PHYLICA pubescens
Flannel Bush

PIERIS formosa var. *forrestii*
Chinese Pearl Flower

PIERIS
(syn ANDROMEDA, AMPELOTHAMNUS)

FRAGRANT

Pearl Flower,
Lily of the Valley Bush

SPRING
SLOW/LONG DISPLAY
HT: 1-3.5m/3-12ft/SPREADING

A relatively small genus (8 species) of Azalea relatives from the colder parts of Asia and North America, *Pieris* are hardy down to −6°C/23°F. They prefer a mildly acid soil that is both well-drained and rich with leaf-mould. A humid atmosphere keeps the evergreen foliage fresh and colourful. In the case of *P. formosa* var. *forestii* the leaves change from scarlet in early spring through cream to a deep, lustrous green in midsummer. Along the way they are joined by panicles of faintly fragrant cream flowers like Lilies of the Valley. This species grows to 4m in height. *P. japonica* is more compact, with leaves (which may be pinkish when young) margined creamy-white in its variety *variegata*. *Pieris* species may be propagated from seed collected in autumn for spring sowing, or from 10cm semi-hardwood tip-cuttings, struck early summer to autumn.

PIERIS japonica variegata
Japanese Andromeda

PIMELEA

Rice Flower

☼ T

SPRING–SUMMER
AVERAGE/LONG DISPLAY
HT: TO 1m/3ft/BUN-SHAPED

Related to European and Asian Daphnes, the fragrant Rice Flowers (*Pimelea* spp.) are an important part of the Australasian flora. There are upwards of 100 species of them scattered across the south of Australia and out to New Zealand—the majority cold-hardy down to −5°C/23°F. *Pimeleas* are easy to strike from semi-hardwood cuttings taken while the plant is in active growth. They must be set out when young, for they will not transplant later. Use them by the coast, or in open, windy places. All they need for success is a light, porous soil, plenty of leaf-mould and sunshine in abundance. Flowers are borne in small terminal umbels, enclosed by colourful bracts. All are short lived.

PIMELEA ferruginea
Pink Rice Flower

PITTOSPORUM

Mockorange

☼ T

SUMMER
AVERAGE/LONG DISPLAY
HT: TO 5m/15ft/STIFF, BUSHY

The many species of *Pittosporum* (over 1000 of them) are perhaps more widely grown in the southern hemisphere than the north. Mostly trees, they are greatly valued for their glossy, laurel-like leaves, clusters of fragrant Daphne-like flowers, and sticky orange fruit. The one great exception is the Japanese *P. tobira* or Mockorange, which is a stiff, bushy evergreen shrub of many uses. It is reasonably frost hardy, can be grown easily from scarified seed in spring, or from half-ripe lateral cuttings taken with a heel in summer. While it will grow to 5m left to its own devices, it can easily be kept more compact with regular pruning. It also shears into a neat hedge and makes a salt-resistant beach or poolside planting. Fragrant creamy blossom in abundance makes a great summer display, and the CV 'Variegata' is effective all year with white-edged grey-green leaves.

PITTOSPORUM tobira
Japanese Pittosporum

PLUMBAGO

☼ ◑ T

Leadwort

SUMMER–WINTER
AVERAGE/LONG DISPLAY
HT: TO 3m/10ft/LOOSE, SPREADING

Only one factor prevents more of us from growing the lovely *Plumbago*—and that's an acute lack of space. For it suckers heavily, and quickly becomes untidy unless cut right back in spring and autumn. You can really only consider using it as an informal hedge, or to disguise ugly walls and fences, for it will climb a little way. Once established (and it is easy to start from cuttings) it is hardy down to −3°C/27°F and remarkably drought and cold resistant. One of those plants with a curious *sticky* feel about it, *Plumbago auriculata* produces lavish clusters of sky-blue phlox-flowers all through the warm weather. Any soil will do provided the drainage is good.

PLUMBAGO auriculata
Cape Plumbago

PODALYRIA FRAGRANT

Sweetpea Bush,
Keurtjie

☼ T

WINTER–SPRING
SLOW/LONG DISPLAY
HT: 2-3m/7-10ft/ROUNDED

Not particularly common away from South Africa, the spring-blooming Sweetpea Bush or *Podalyria calyptrata* is a most useful shrub in exposed positions. Always decorative, *Podalyria* is evergreen—or to be more accurate, evergrey, for its leaves are covered in white, silvery hair which shines in the sunlight. The pea flowers, which are very fragrant, are usually a soft mauve-pink, though there are colour variations. Grow it from seed, which must be soaked 24 hours in hot water before sowing, or from soft tip-cuttings taken in warm weather.

A gravelly, well-drained soil is best with heavy regular water over the winter months. Young plants should be tip-pruned to encourage compactness; flowered shoots should be reduced by half on older specimens. *Podalyria* is reasonably drought resistant, and cold hardy down to −3°C/27°F.

PODALYRIA calyptrata
Sweetpea Bush

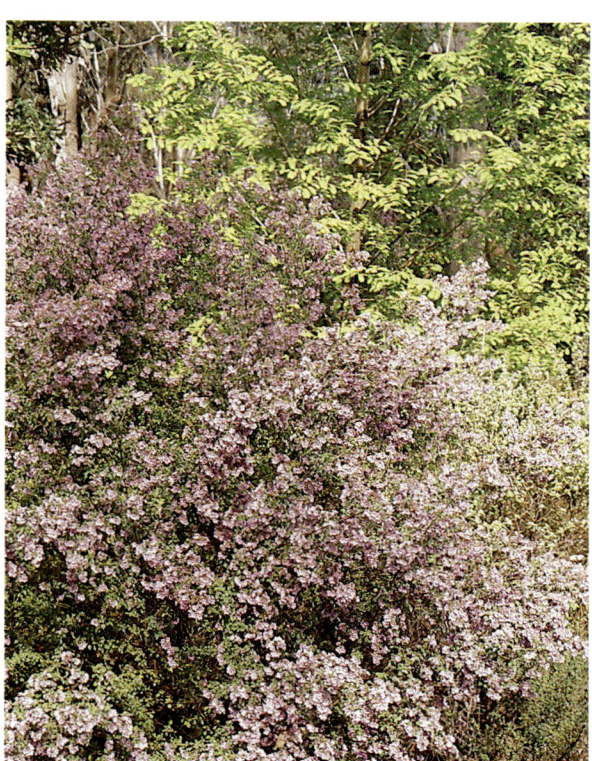

PROSTANTHERA *baxteri*
Silver Mint Bush

PROSTANTHERA

Mint Bush

SPRING–SUMMER
AVERAGE/SHORT DISPLAY
HT: 1-3m/3-10ft

Short-lived but splashy flowering shrubs, Australia's aromatic Mint Bushes (*Prostanthera* spp.) bloom mostly in shades of mauve and harmonize perfectly with Prunus, Cornus and other treasures of the spring garden. Grow them in a sheltered position anywhere the soil is gravelly, well-drained and rich in leaf-mould. They can be propagated from firm tip-cuttings taken in summer or autumn and struck in moist, gritty sand. Longer-lived plants can be produced by grafting *Prostanthera* scions onto stock from the Australian Westringia which is more resistant to root rot. All species can be compacted by lightly trimming new season's growth after blooming is done. *P. ovalifolia* is the commonest species, but there are about 40 others. They are grown in the western United States, southern U.K., all Mediterranean climates.

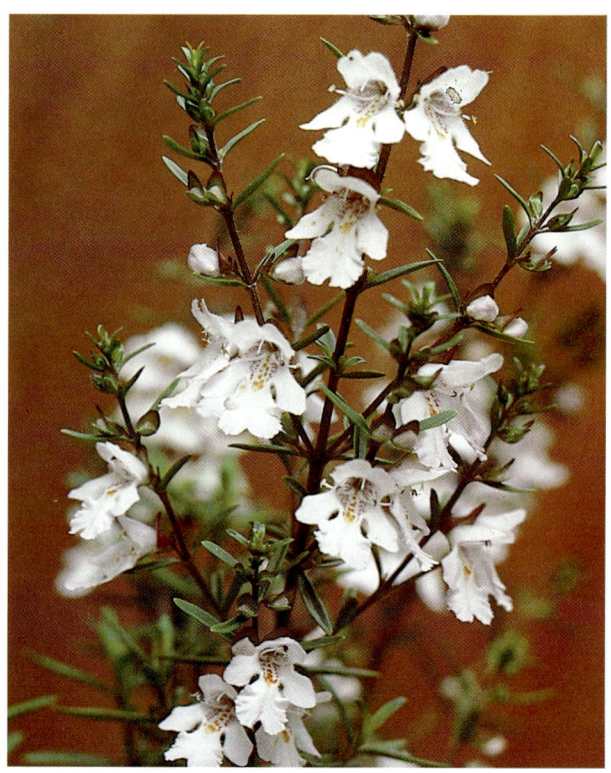

PROSTANTHERA *ovalifolia*
Purple Mint Bush

PROSTANTHERA *saxicola*
Mountain Mintbush

PROTEA HONEY SCENTED

Sugarbush,
Honeyflower

☼ T

AUTUMN–SPRING
SLOW/LONG DISPLAY
HT: 1-3m/3-10ft/SQUAT

Of the many remarkable personalities in Greek mythology, none had a more extraordinary appearance than Proteus, son of the mighty sea-god Poseidon. He had the power of assuming any shape, and might appear at any time as a tree, a snake, a lion or even as fire or water. It was this gift of unlimited shape-changing which suggested the name *Protea* to 18th century botanists classifying a newly discovered and highly variable group of South African plants. They believed them unique, though we now know there are close relatives in South America and also in Australia. The true *Proteas* however will always be associated with South Africa, where one of them has been named as the national flower emblem. There are about 100 species, mostly from the mountainous, sea-girt Cape Province, and they are not too difficult to grow once their needs are clearly understood. Sandy soil is the first rule (preferably acid, though some species will make do with an alkaline pH), perfect drainage the second, (they are well grown on hillsides or in terraced beds), full sun the third. They are slow growers, and relatively short lived, but the beauty of the often gigantic blooms makes every effort seem worthwhile. *Proteas* last well when cut, and as they retain shape after fading, are often saved for dried arrangements. Flower size is not necessarily related to shrub size, by the way. The startling King Protea (*P. cynaroides*) produces 25cm blooms on a 1m bush, and must be staked in case of overbalancing.

Proteas can be raised from autumn or spring-sown seed, but germination is erratic and the resultant seedlings not necessarily true to type. *Proteas*, as a generalization, bear concave, silky leaves clasping tough, woody stems. The compact blooms consist of a number of tubular flowers, surrounded by several rows of highly coloured bracts. All are rich in honey and attractive to birds.

PROTEA neriifolia
Oleander-leaf Protea

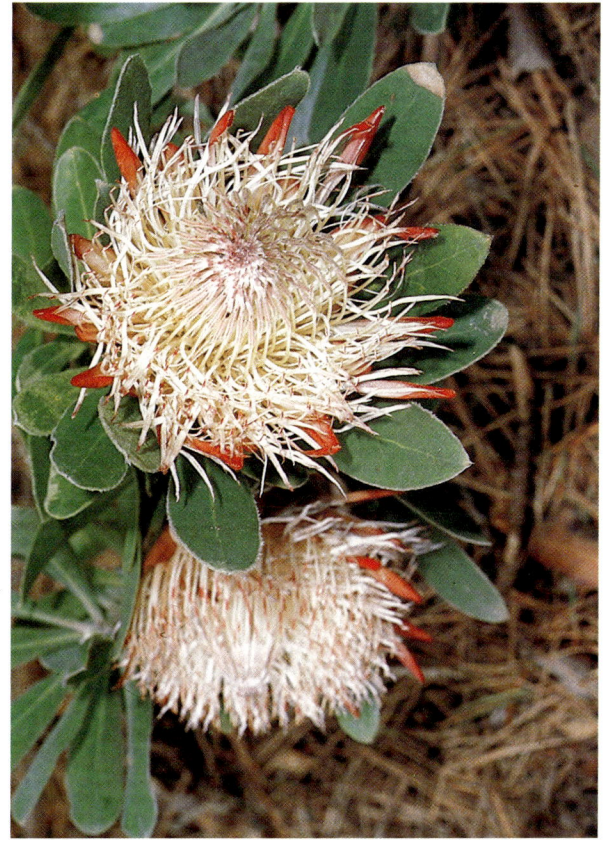

PROTEA susannae
Susan's Protea

PROTEA cynaroides
King Protea

PROTEA barbigera
Giant Woollybeard

PROTEA repens
Sugarbush, Honeyflower

PRUNUS

Flowering Almond Cherry,
Bush Cherry

WINTER–SPRING
FAST/SHORT DISPLAY
HT: 1m/3ft/SUCKERING

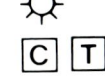

With a rich assortment of *Prunus* species available among the wealth of flowering trees, it's nice to know there are also several among the shrubs. Mostly they are cultivars of the illustrated Chinese Bush Cherry, *P. glandulosa,* a dainty, suckering shrub generally less than a metre high. There are single and double CVs, both with white or pink flowers. All are deciduous, and colour brightly in autumn. They are easy to propagate from divisions, and single varieties only can be propagated from seed. Spreading of the parent plant can be forced by cutting back flowered stems to the ground. A rich neutral to alkaline soil is best, and moisture should be applied regularly through spring and summer. A year-round mulch is helpful.

PRUNUS glandulosa
Chinese Bush Cherry

PSEUDERANTHEMUM
(*syn ERANTHEMUM*)

Golden Net Bush,
Eldorado

ALL YEAR ROUND
AVERAGE/CONTINUOUS DISPLAY
HT: 1-1.8m/3-6ft

You'll find *Pseuderanthemums* difficult to grow without a minimum winter temperature of 13°C/55°F. Only one of 60-odd species is seen in cultivation: *P. reticulatum,* the Golden Net Bush, from Vanuatu (formerly the New Hebrides). It has golden stems and bright yellow leaves with a network of green lines, although in partly shaded positions it tends to settle for a greener tone. The shrub is generally erect and bushy, and where the climate is warm enough, bloom is continuous. This consists of dainty, carmine-spotted white blooms borne in panicles, both at leaf axils and at branch tips. But mostly it is grown as a foliage plant and trimmed regularly to a compact shape. Rich, well-drained soil is necessary, with regular water and fertilizer. Grow from warm weather cuttings.

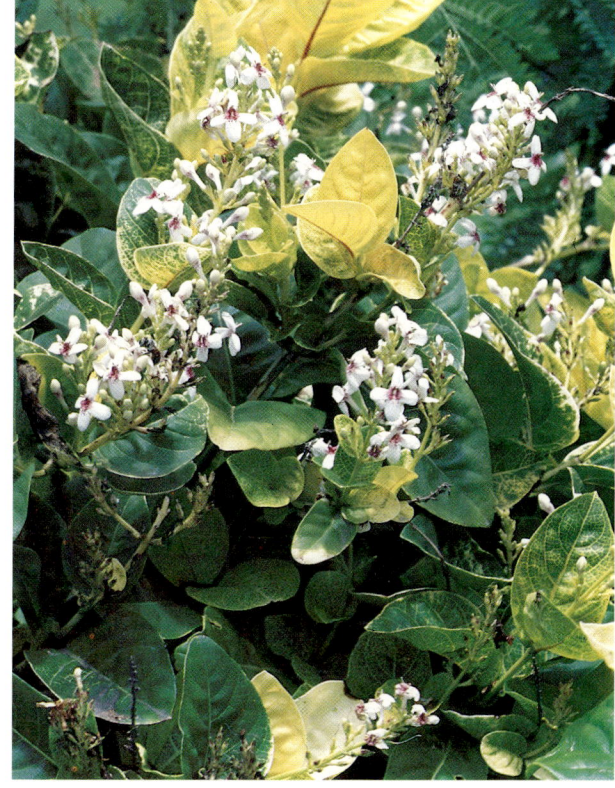

PSEUDERANTHEMUM reticulatum
Golden Net Bush

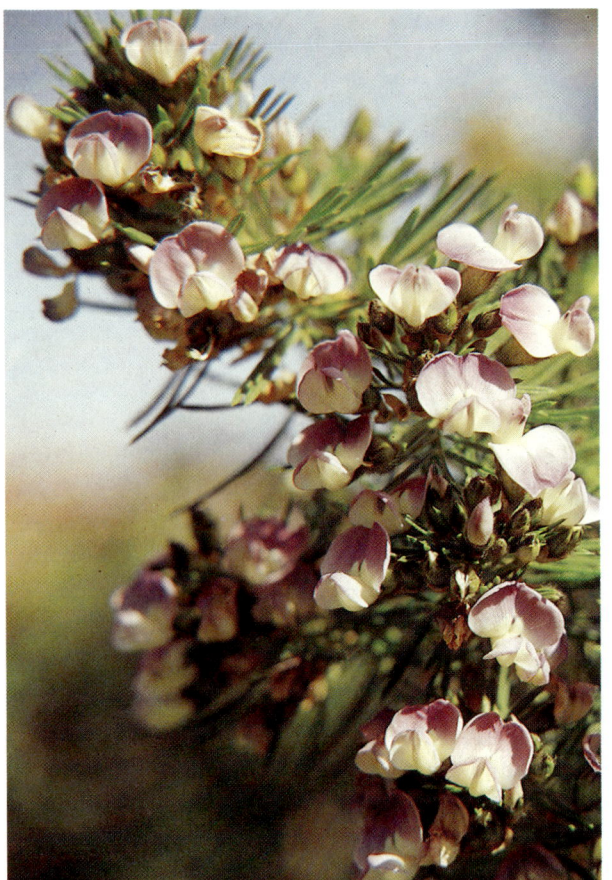

PSORALEA

Blue Butterfly Bush

SPRING
FAST/LONG DISPLAY
HT: 1-1.8m/4-6ft/BUSHY

Psoraleas are fast-growing, shrubby members of the pea family with heath-like leaves and blue, white or purple flowers. There are representative species on almost every continent and generally they do well in a light, sandy soil (even on the poor side); they are barely frost-tender. They may be grown from seed, which ripens in summer and autumn, or from spring cuttings of half-ripened shoots which should be struck in a sandy mixture with warmth and humidity. Popular *Psoralea pinnata* should be pruned back heavily after bloom to prevent its adopting a leggy, tree-like shape. Otherwise it will need a heavy planting of tall perennials or smaller shrubs in front to disguise the bare-trunked appearance. Flowers are attractively shaded mauve and white.

PSORALEA pinnata
Blue Butterfly Bush

PSYCHOTRIA FRAGRANT

Wild Coffee

SPRING
AVERAGE/LONG DISPLAY
HT: TO 1m/3ft/COMPACT

Related to Bouvardia, Gardenia, Ixora, Luculia and other beautiful warm climate shrubs, the *Psychotrias* have been relegated to the status of also-rans. They have many good features: glossy foliage, dense terminal clusters of pink, white or yellow flowers (small it's true, but very fragrant) and a colourful crop of berries to follow. But that's just not enough when it comes to the fierce competition for space in the warm climate garden. So most of them (there are up to 700 species) remain local favourites in their home territories, which could be South or Central America, Africa, the Caribbean, or even Fiji. They can be grown from the seed of dried berries, or from cuttings struck under heat. Brilliantly coloured *P. capensis* from Africa is occasionally seen in other areas with similar climates.

PSYCHOTRIA capensis
Wild Coffee

PUNICA

Pomegranate

SPRING–SUMMER
FAST/LONG DISPLAY
HT: TO 1m/3ft/DENSE

With the smaller scale of modern gardens, every plant has to earn its place. So the larger growing Pomegranate varieties are rarely seen now, outside the Middle East. We have found more fragrant flowers, more edible fruits, to take their place. Contrariwise, the Dwarf Pomegranate, *Punica granatum nana,* is more widely seen every day. Rarely more than a metre high or wide, it produces dainty miniatures of the larger Pomegranate flowers and fruit throughout the warmer weather. Grow it in a coarse, gravelly soil, reward it with occasional water and prune lightly every year to keep compact. *Punica* will resist heat and drought to a great degree, yet is hardy down to −8°C/17°F.

PUNICA granatum nana
Dwarf Pomegranate

RAPHIOLEPIS   FRAGRANT

Indian or Yedo Hawthorn

WINTER–SUMMER
SLOW/LONG DISPLAY
HT: 1-3m/3-9ft

Most useful and attractive of shrubs, the two species and many cultivars of *Raphiolepis* can be relied on for spring display in all climates from cold to warm temperate. Cold-hardy down to −9°C/15°F with only minor leaf damage, they also thrive close to the sea in salt air and sandy soil, and are a problem only in dry, desert areas, where the beautiful foliage can be badly desiccated; there they need semi-shade protection.

Although *Raphiolepis* grow readily from seed, which is collected when ripe in autumn, they will normally save you the trouble and produce seedlings far and wide in the vicinity of the parent plant. These young plants, however, may not be true to

RAPHIOLEPIS indica
Indian Hawthorn

type. A more reliable method is to take cuttings of half-ripened tips during autumn and winter and strike them in a warm, humid place.

All types of *Raphiolepis* do best in a rich, well-drained soil, and need lots of water through spring and summer. They will produce numerous spreading branches from a single short trunk, and shape can be controlled by pruning. Sweet-scented *R. indica* has slightly toothed leaves and sprays of delicate pink bloom followed by black berries. More commonly seen Yedo Hawthorn (*R. umbellata*) has leathery simple leaves, red-centred white flowers in packed clusters. It may bloom the entire year. Both feature red-tinted new foliage.

RAPHIOLEPIS umbellata
Yedo Hawthorn

RAPHIOLEPIS 'Springtime'
Hybrid

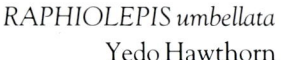

REINWARDTIA
(syn LINUM)

Yellow Flax

☼ T

AUTUMN–WINTER
AVERAGE/LONG DISPLAY
HT: TO 1m/3ft/SUCKERING

Coarse, untidy plants that light up the cold weather with brilliant golden flowers, *Reinwardtias* are grown from winter division or from soft tip-cuttings taken in spring. A light, well-drained soil is best, and *Reinwardtias* should be attempted in warm-winter districts only. They look well in semi-shade, but the flowers show up best in full sun, provided an ample water supply can be laid on. Mature plants are inclined to grow leggy, and should be pinched out regularly to force branching. Encourage the formation of a dense clump by chopping the whole plant back to half height in late winter. Yellow Flax is an evergreen, though sparsely-foliaged plant with rather soft, simple leaves. It can make a showy container plant.

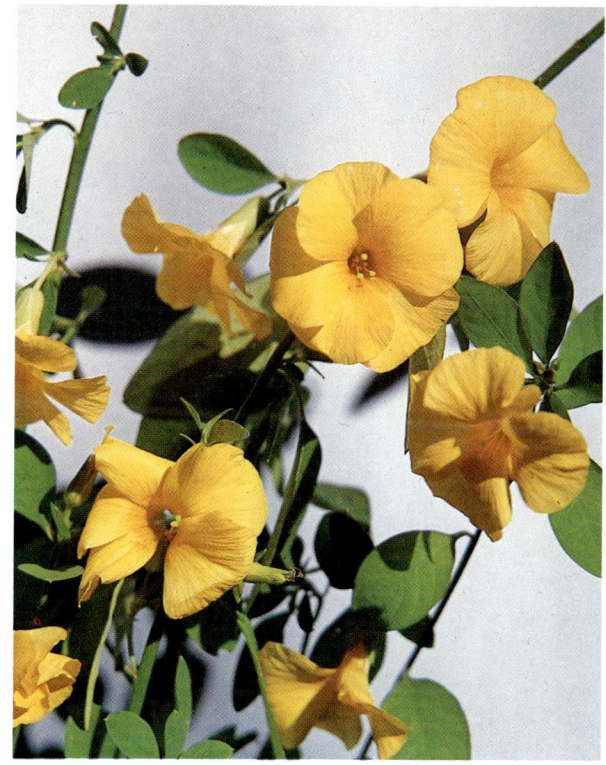
REINWARDTIA indica
Yellow Flax

RETAMA
(syn GENISTA)　　　　FRAGRANT

White Weeping Broom

☼ T

WINTER–SPRING
FAST/LONG DISPLAY
HT: 2-3m/6-10ft/WEEPING

A short-trunked plant with weeping stems that are almost leafless, *Retama monosperma* is found all about the Mediterranean. Resistant to both heat and cold (it thrives down to −3°C/27°F), *Retama* seems to do well anywhere the humidity is not too high. It is propagated almost exclusively from seed, a relatively simple process. Just collect in autumn, store in a cool, dry place and sow in pots of sandy mix the following spring after a 24 hour soak in warm water. Set the seedlings out in a well-drained, gravelly soil, water lightly and stand back. *Retama's* white pea flowers, borne profusely along the silvery stems in spring, have a sweet, almost cloying fragrance. Prune lightly after bloom.

RETAMA monosperma
White Weeping Broom

RHODODENDRON

Tree Rose

SPRING–SUMMER
AVERAGE/SHORT DISPLAY
HT: 10-600cm/4-240in

Assuming such a visit to be possible, a garden fancier from the mid 19th century might well be struck dumb with amazement on visiting a modern *Rhododendron* nursery. For almost every plant he saw would be quite unfamiliar. There would be new flower forms, new colours, new habits of growth, new fragrances. Many of the plants might even be unrecognizable to him as Rhododendrons at all, so great has been the change in this beautiful genus of plants.

No much over a century ago, gardeners of Europe and North America were limited to only a few species from mountain areas of their own coun-tries. Perhaps 15 species were known in all, as opposed to the 500 and more grown today. And that is only *species*—modern hybrids between them would number several thousand at least.

The *Rhododendron* is a perfect example of supply and demand as applied to horticulture. The later 19th century saw the rise of the great private estate as the newly-rich captains of industry vied with the aristocracy in creating their private pleasure domes surrounded by park-like gardens. They engaged designers and landscape construction teams who in turn sought out ever more spectacular plants to furnish their demesnes. There was such big money to be made that many larger nurseries commissioned plant hunters to explore and bring back new plant species from all over the globe. One of the great success stories of that era was *Rhododendron,* whose species were discovered by the hundred in China, Tibet and Assam.

Today, among all flowering shrub genera, the majestic *Rhododendrons* must surely reign supreme

RHODODENDRON X *loderi*

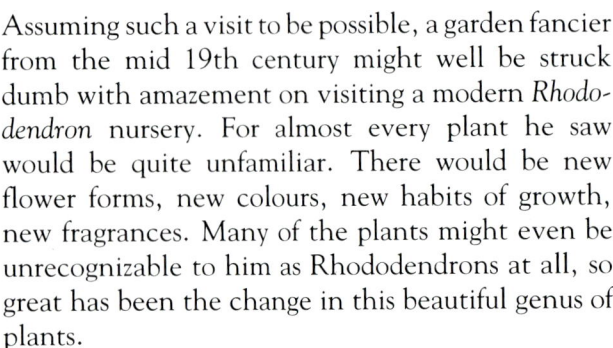

RHODODENDRON lochae
Queensland Tree Rose

RHODODENDRON X'Fragrantissimum'

RHODODENDRON augustinii
Blue Rhododendron

RHODODENDRON X 'Eldorado'

for the sheer size, brilliance and profusion of their flowers. Most types produce enormous trusses of bloom in a colour range no other plant genus can rival. Even out of bloom they are attractive, densely clothed with dark, evergreen leaves.

But there's a catch. *Rhododendrons* won't grow just anywhere. They are native to and do best in places where winters are cool to cold, springs cool and moist, summers warm and humid. They grow to perfection in many parts of England and Ireland, in the western United States, in New Zealand and in the mountain tablelands of eastern Austrālia. *Rhododendrons* do best with protection from hot afternoon sun and strong winds—especially hot *drying* winds. They stay fresh in the rising humidity

RHODODENDRON X
'President Roosevelt'

RHODODENDRON X
'Countess of Haddington'

RHODODENDRON X 'Koster's Red'

RHODODENDRON X
·Yvonne Opaline'

below tall trees. Generally speaking, the cooler the climate, the more ·sun is tolerated, especially in winter. Full shade all day results in disappointing flowers, but in coastal areas shade is beneficial·on summer afternoons. Soil should be water-retentive, yet porous enough to allow excess water to drain freely. A light, sandy loam enriched with well-rotted compost or leaf-mould is suitable. *Rhododen-drons* detest lime, and must have an acid soil with a pH of between 5 and 6.

Keep the plants consistently moist, but never wet. Keep the air moisture as high as possible, mulch annually with compost to save water and feed the surface roots.

Rhododendrons hybridize easily, so do not come true from seed. Propagate them vegetatively from spring layers lifted in autumn, or from 12cm semi-hardwood cuttings. These should be taken from early summer to mid-autumn, and struck in a gritty mix with warmth and humidity.

Because of their mountain origins, many *Rhodo-dendrons* are perfectly cold hardy and will withstand temperatures well below 0°C/32°F. Your local nurseryman will advise the best species for your area.

RHODODENDRON *ponticum*

RIBES

Flowering Currant

WINTER–SPRING
FAST/LONG DISPLAY
HT: 1.5-3m/4½-10ft/VARIABLE

Though they are not the fruiting currants of the kitchen garden, these *Ribes* species certainly look good enough to eat. They are of course members of the same genus, which includes around 150 species in all, mostly native to the Americas, but with some found in other parts of the northern hemisphere. The illustrated species are favourite shrubs for cooler climate gardens, producing masses of spicily fragrant bloom, mostly on spiny stems. They can be grown from hardwood cuttings taken in late winter, though these are slow to root. They are deciduous, have lobed leaves, grow best in well-drained soil with an annual top-dressing in spring. *R. aureum* and *R. speciosum* defoliate unless watering is continued in summer. *R. sanguineum* prefers a cool, moist climate and is hardy down to −10°C/14°F.

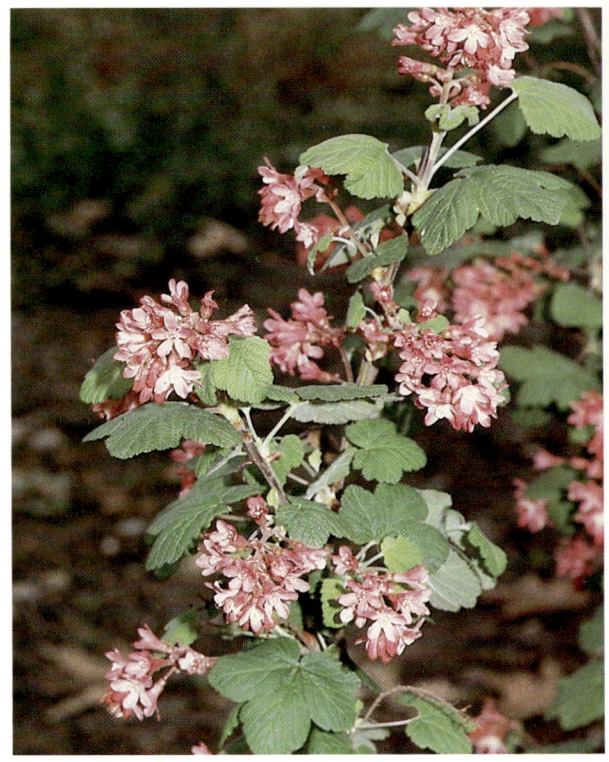

RIBES sanguineum
Red Flowering Currant

RIBES aureum
Golden Currant

RIBES speciosum
California Fuchsia

RONDELETIA odorata
Sweet-scented Rondeletia

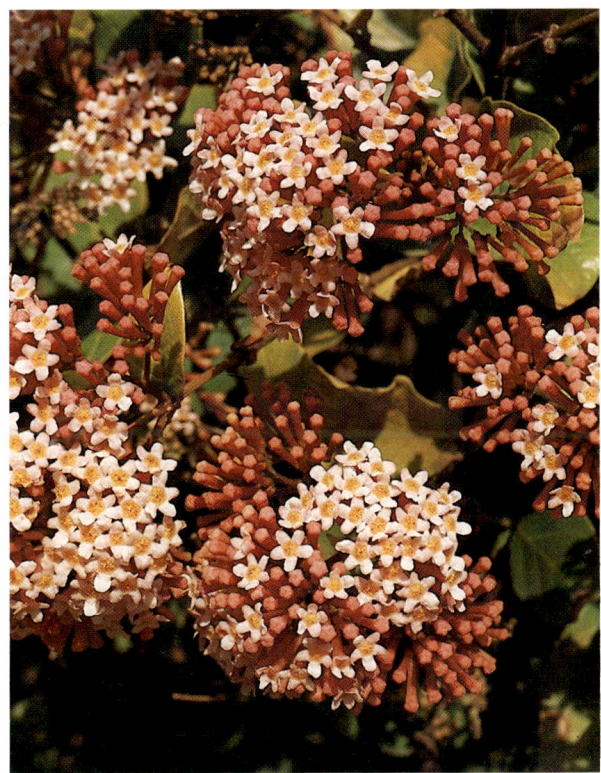

RONDELETIA amoena
Rondeletia

RONDELETIA strigosa
Hairy Rondeletia

RONDELETIA FRAGRANT

Rondeletia

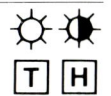

SPRING–AUTUMN
AVERAGE/SHORT DISPLAY
HT: 1-3m/3-10ft/VARIABLE

These generally fragrant and colourful flowering shrubs hail from the Caribbean, where they give a continuous display. However, as none of them is cold hardy, their flowering period becomes shorter the further away they are from the tropics. In cooler temperate areas they must be grown under glass with winter heat. *Rondeletias* do best in a soil that is barely acid and well-drained, need uniform moisture through the warmer months. Most commonly seen *R. amoena* and *R. odorata* can be raised from 10cm semi-hardwood tip-cuttings taken in late spring and struck indoors under warm humid conditions. *R. strigosa*, which has a suckering habit, is more easily raised from divisions. All are evergreen and improve with an annual light pruning.

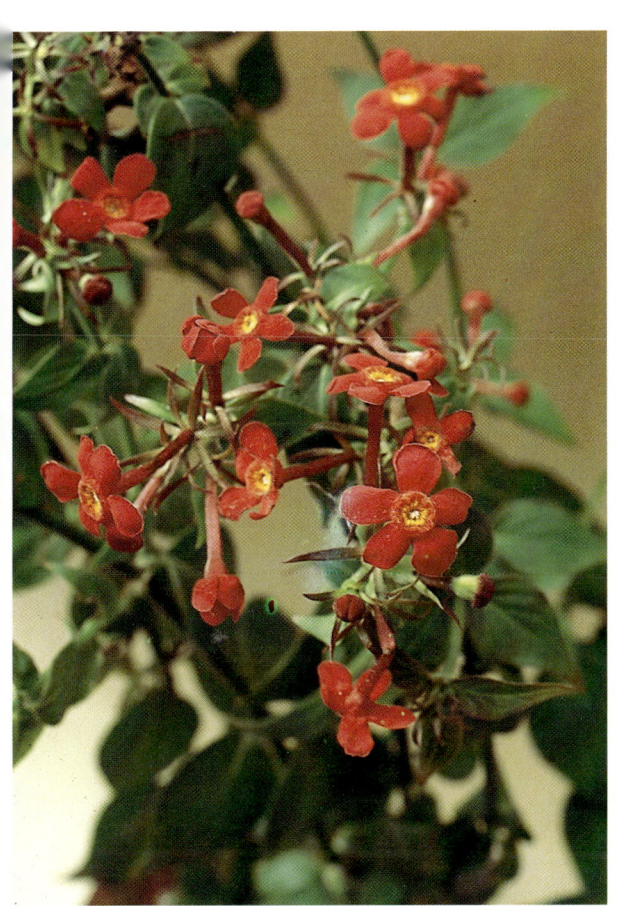

ROSA

FRAGRANT

Rose

SPRING–AUTUMN
FAST/INTERMITTENT DISPLAY
HT: 60-900cm/2-30ft/VARIABLE

Roses of one sort or another have been in cultivation for at least 5000 years, making them the best-loved flower in history. The Chinese, we know from old books, grew them around 3000 B.C. Several millenia later, the Greeks had a word for them, *Rhodos*, and gave that name to the Mediterranean island of Rhodes, where they grew to perfection. Greek poets Sappho and Anacreon hailed the rose as queen of flowers.

Later still, the Romans prized these flowers for their fragrance, enjoying them at banquets, as both a delicacy and a dedication to Venus, their goddess of love. Cleopatra spent over sixty pounds weight of gold to buy rose petals for the famous banquet where she seduced Mark Antony. They carpeted the decks of her galley 20 inches thick beneath a golden net.

Roman historian Pliny describes twelve varieties of rose that were cultivated in Rome. Some are still grown, but now take second place to the beauties raised by modern hybridists. New rose species introduced from Persia and India, from China and North America, brought with them yellow, pink, bronze and cerise colourings, and the continuous flowering habit we take so much for granted. The ancients knew roses only as red or white, and could look forward to their blooming only at the height of summer.

Roses are now grown all around the world, though wild species occur only north of the equator. There they grow naturally in the temperate zone of all continents, although some species have adapted to life almost on the edge of the tropics. Such a one is the Burmese *Rosa gigantea*, a parent of 'Nancy Hayward' illustrated on page 152. This is one of a limited number of roses suited to warmer climates.

Generally speaking, roses are at their best in areas with mildly alkaline soil of clay texture, though many patient growers have succeeded in raising prize-winning blooms in acid soil and have even adapted sand to a suitable tilth.

ROSA X 'F.J.Grootendorst'
Hybrid Ramanas Rose

Over 250 wild species have been identified, and almost all of them have now been used by hybridists to produce the rainbow of blooms available to us today. An entire book could be written on cultural directions for varying climates, and your local nurseryman is the best adviser for where you live.

In warm temperate climates, roses are planted in midwinter, and normally pruned at the same time, except for winter flowering types. Where winters are harder, they are normally planted in autumn, given a heavy mulch over the root system, and pruned when signs of new growth appear in spring.

Roses enjoy full sun, especially in the morning, and do best in a bed of their own, well away from marauding tree roots, and without competition from annuals and other plants. They need regular feeding, and exhaust the soil so completely that they leave it in a condition known as 'rose sick'. A new rose should never be planted where one has been grown before without complete replacement of the soil over an area 1m square and as deep as the root system.

Regular watering is essential and a deep surface mulch around the root areas will help produce top-

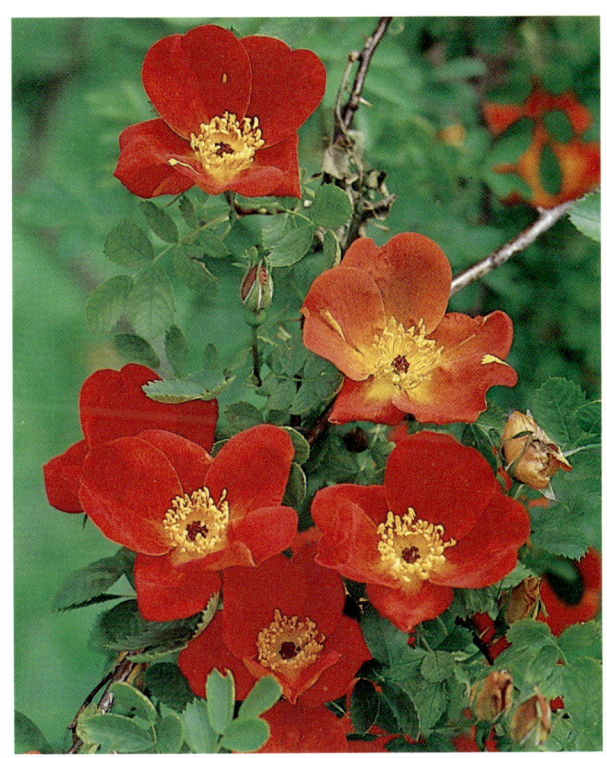

ROSA foetida bicolor
Austrian Copper Briar

ROSA sinica alba
Cherokee Rose

ROSA 'Picasso'
Floribunda Rose

quality blooms. While 9 out of 10 rose plants bought today are of the 'hybrid tea' or 'floribunda' types, many of the original species are coming back into fashion. They do not flower as continuously as the modern hybrids, but have a beauty and fragrance all of their own.

PESTS AND DISEASES

Roses are no more prone to attack by pests and diseases than any other group of plants, but their blooms are normally so perfect that any sign of damage stands out.

Aphids are the most obvious of pests, though probably the least serious. They crowd new growth of foliage and flower buds, sucking tasty juices and often leaving distortion in their wake. Blast them away with the hose or check with any spray formulated for sucking insects.

Grasshoppers of various kinds often chew at foliage, and flower buds may be holed by *caterpillars* of several kinds. A systemic insecticide is more effective here. Prune away damaged foliage or buds.

Fungus diseases of several kinds may become apparent, particularly in humid weather. Most serious is *powdery mildew* which is deposited as a thin, white coating on new foliage, causing it to distort. Spraying with a recommended fungicide will normally wipe it out, but the damaged foliage should be pruned away and burned.

Black spot is most clearly described by its popular name. Mature foliage becomes spotted with black or dark brown blotches which rapidly increase in size. Leaves finally turn yellow and drop. All affected foliage should be cut and burned and the affected plant sprayed with a reliable fungicide. Difficult to cure completely, but in the long run the plant does not seem to be unduly damaged provided regular hygiene is practised.

Finally, a fungus infection known as *die-back* may enter the plant's sap system through pruning cuts. All dead wood should be cut away with sterilized secateurs and large cuts sealed with a bitumen pruning compound.

Rose plants are such good value, as a result of mass production, that hardly anyone bothers to propagate their own. It is quite practicable, however, to raise them from cuttings, taken in midsummer. An elderly cousin of mine has been doing it for many years, and has raised a fine collection of roses as a result.

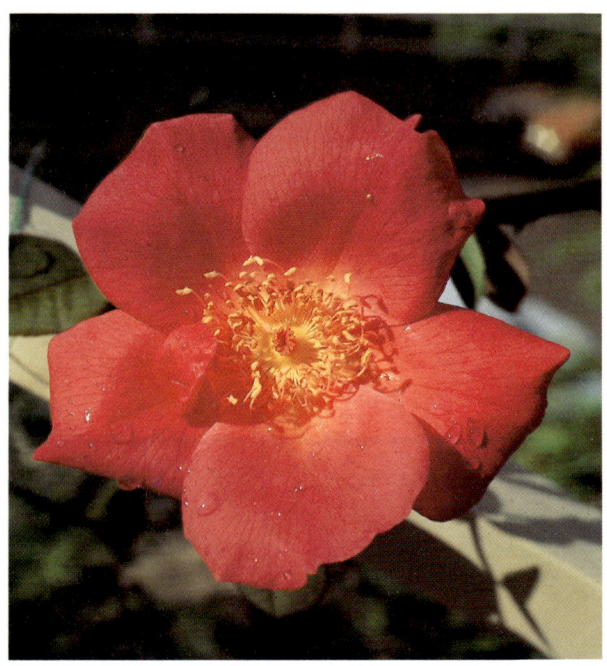

ROSA 'Nancy Hayward'
Gigantea Hybrid

ROSA 'Princess Michael of Kent'
Hybrid Tea Rose

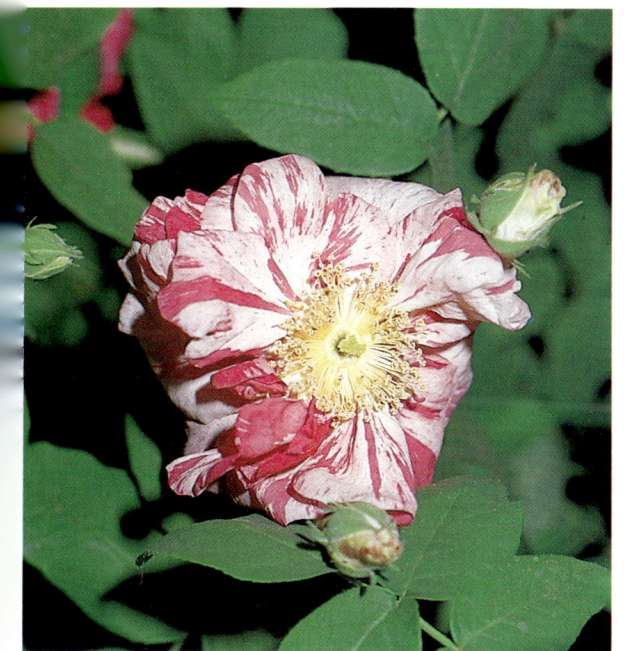

ROSA gallica versicolor
Rosa Mundi

ROSA 'Baronne de Prévost'
Hybrid Perpetual Rose

ROSA X *harisonii*
Harison's Yellow Rose

RUELLIA

Christmas Pride

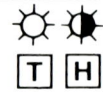

WINTER–SPRING
AVERAGE/LONG DISPLAY
HT: 1.5-2m/5-7ft/VASE-SHAPED

Useful only where winter temperatures can be kept above 13°C/55°F, *Ruellias* are so lovely they are often kept as winter-flowering greenhouse plants in the northern hemisphere. In milder areas, they are grown from spring cuttings, continuously pinched back to ensure bushy growth. Give them semi-shade through the hottest weather, plenty of water, and a periodic application of liquid fertilizer to hurry growth along.

    Ruellia macrantha (one of about 200 species) needs as much winter sun as it can get to force flower production. Blooms are about 6cm in diameter, quilted in texture and coloured a delicious violet-pink. Prune them back by all means, but the best display will come from newly struck autumn cuttings. A fibrous, well-drained soil is best.

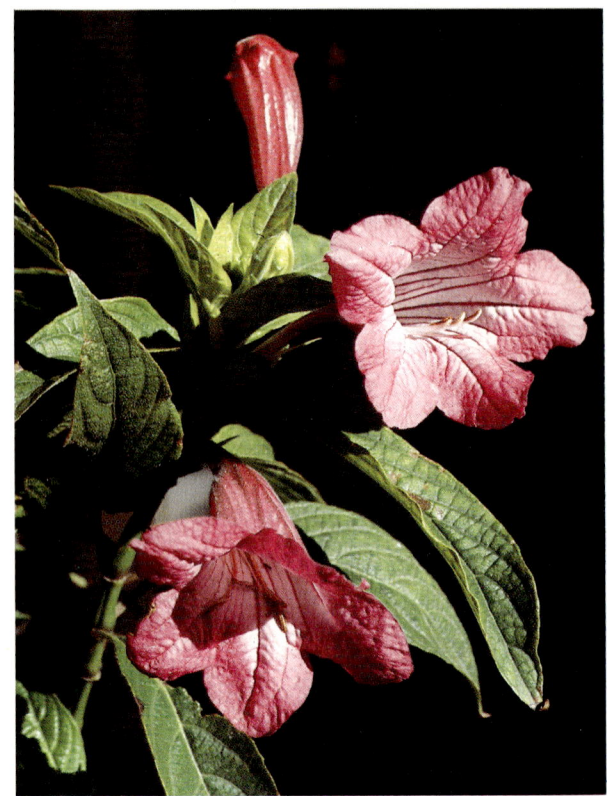

RUELLIA *macrantha*
Christmas Pride

RUSSELIA

Coral Blow,
Fountain Plant

SPRING–AUTUMN
FAST/LONG DISPLAY
HT: 60-100cm/2-4ft/FOUNTAIN-SHAPED

Another Central American beauty; and wouldn't you know it from the lush, warm-weather growth, the profusion of scarlet flowers like fire-crackers at a Mexican fiesta! *Russelia* is a true horticultural celebration, turning from a tangled mess of leafless cold-weather growth to a glowing fountain of coral-scarlet in summer. It likes a moderately rich, well-drained soil, and is not hard to grow from cuttings. It grows fast, spreads rapidly into a stand of arching, sucker-like stems on which the foliage has been modified to tiny scales. The Coral Blow is a good seaside plant, or effective spilling over a bank or wall. Best results are stimulated by a light pruning of spent flower heads in winter, at which time some old stems can be taken right back to the base. Hardy down to −2°C/28°F.

RUSSELIA *juncea*
Coral Blow

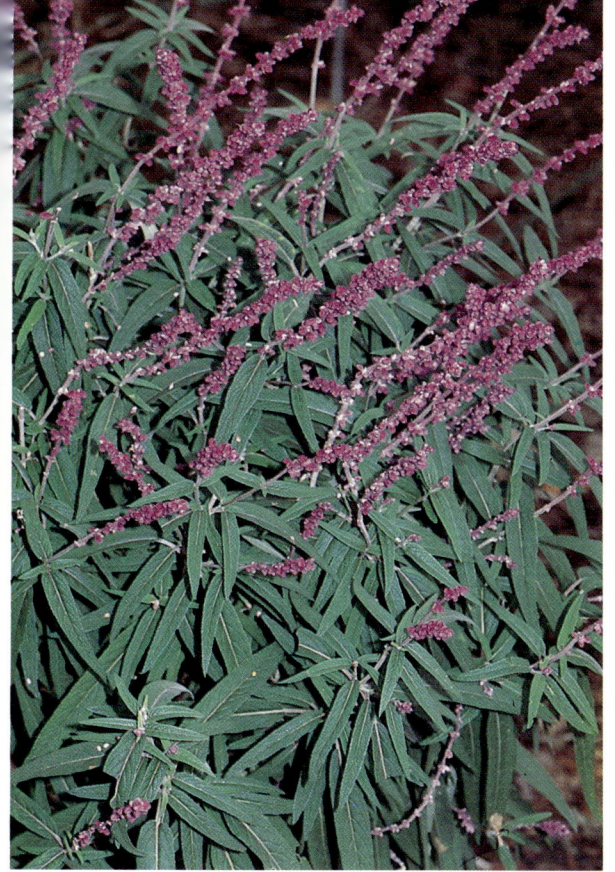

SALVIA leucantha
Mexican Bush Sage

SALVIA AROMATIC

Sage

AROUND AUTUMN
AVERAGE/LONG DISPLAY
HT: 60-100cm/2-4ft/
    IRREGULARLY SPREADING

Early explorers credited Mexican Aztecs with the most dazzling flower displays ever seen, but I sometimes wonder whether their modern descendants have inherited a love of gardens at all. Judging by the range of gorgeous plants found only within Mexico's borders, the whole place should look like a living rainbow, but from the movies one sees . . . Anyway, you'd certainly have to go a long way to find any bloom as vividly purple as the Mexican Bush Sage at left. One of nearly 500 sage species, it enjoys a rich soil and is easy to strike from 7cm cuttings of non-flowering lateral shoots or from divisions. The whole plant has a velvety feel and is aromatic in all its parts. It is drought resistant and should be cut back hard in late winter.

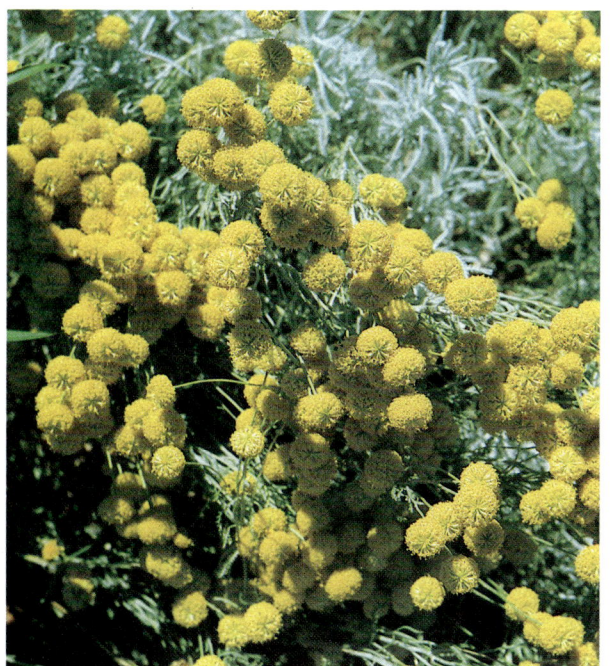

SANTOLINA chamaecyparissus
Lavender Cotton

SANTOLINA AROMATIC

Lavender Cotton

SUMMER
FAST/ALWAYS DECORATIVE
HT: 60cm/2ft/MOUNDED

Delicate foliage like feather dusters has brought *Santolina* a special place in the mixed border or rockery, and it is usually clipped back into a neat mound in early spring. But that is only half its beauty. Left untrained, it will produce masses of yellow button-flowers in summer. *Santolinas* of any species (there are 8) are hardy except in frost, are all found naturally around the Mediterranean area. But as gardeners have discovered, they will grow any place there is sun and water. Grow from seed, cuttings or layers. Try them in a light, sandy soil, with occasional but regular water. Tip-prune frequently and shear off all spent flowers. Replace with cuttings when woodiness becomes apparent.

SENECIO

Groundsel

DIFFERENT SEASONS/ALL YEAR
FAST/LONG DISPLAY
HT: 1-5m/3-15ft

The enormous variety of daisy-flowered plants called *Senecio* makes up one of the largest genera in the vegetable kingdom. There are over 1300 of them, found literally on every continent, though the best species originate from South Africa and the western areas of both American continents. The most popular and useful shrubby types include Mexico's enormous *S. grandifolius*, which has dark 50cm leaves and trusses of bright yellow daisy flowers in cold weather. New Zealand's *S. laxifolius* has small simple greyish leaves and a spreading habit, while the California Geranium, *S. petasites*, has handsome lobed foliage and sparsely petalled flowers in great panicles. All grow from cuttings, need annual pruning.

SENECIO grandifolius
Big-leaf Groundsel

SENECIO laxifolius
Dusty Miller

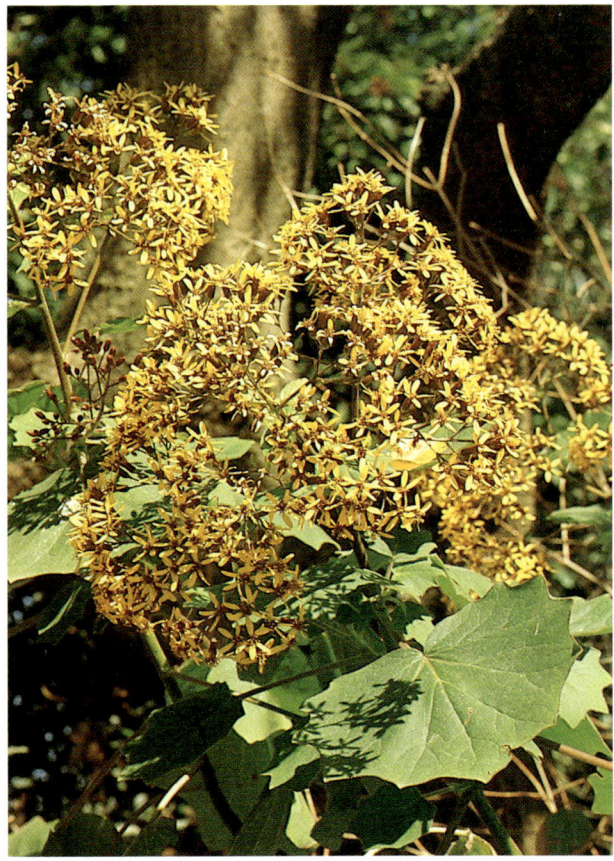

SENECIO petasites
California Geranium

SKIMMIA

(no popular name)

☼ ☀
T

SPRING
SLOW/LONG DISPLAY
HT: 1-1.5m/3-5ft/DENSELY MOUNDED

Just a handful of species from cooler parts of Asia,
the *Skimmias* are related to Citrus, and to the
fragrant Murraya or Mockorange, which they replace
in gardens of cooler climates. *S. japonica* is most
commonly seen, in town gardens and in parks, for it
is remarkably resistant to polluted city air. Tiny
creamy flowers join the shining evergreen foliage in
spring, and if you've the right planting combination
(you need both male and female bushes) you'll get a
crop of persistent bright-red berries in late summer.
A well-drained acid soil is best, with generous moisture in dry weather. As the bushes remain compact
and tidy, little pruning is needed, but cuttings may
be taken in summer and struck with heat.

SKIMMIA *japonica*
in spring blossom

SOLANUM

Potato Bush

☼ T

SPRING–SUMMER
FAST/LONG DISPLAY
HT: 1.8-2.3m/6-8ft/UNTIDY

Another enormous and most variable genus of
plants, the *Solanums* are found all over the world,
though mostly in warmer climates. They include
climbers, annuals and a tree or two, as well as many
food plants such as the eggplant and potato. Most
however, are grown purely for the beauty of their
floral display, though it must be confessed fragrance
is something of a rarity among them. Illustrated
species *S. rantonettii* is most variable, seen sometimes as a medium-sized shrub, sometimes as a vine
or even a sprawling groundcover. It is from South
America, not frost hardy and is best grown from soft
tip-cuttings struck in warm weather. Heavy pruning
is needed to keep it shapely—but just look at the end
result!

SOLANUM *rantonettii*
Blue Potato Bush

SPARTIUM

Spanish Broom

SPRING–SUMMER
FAST/LONG DISPLAY
HT: 1-2.3m/3-8ft/SPARSE

The longtime favourite Spanish Broom stands out anywhere, with masses of canary-yellow pea flowers blooming throughout the late spring and early summer. I like to remember it in the south of France, rolled out along the highways like a golden carpet, welcoming the well-heeled tourist to the Côte d'Azur—but in fact it's an easy plant to grow anywhere the sun is mildly warm. Don't worry about the type of soil, it seems happy even in poor stony stuff, or fast-draining coastal sand. If it has a preference, it is for a little lime to sweeten its growth along. *Spartium junceum* is almost leafless, a mass of hollow, straw-like green twigs springing from a crowded base. And if you want it to do anything but sprawl, you must prune heavily after blooming, right into the old wood. You can use it as a hedge or deep ground cover, even as a seaside planting. In windy places, though, give it some support, for it is inclined to be shallow rooted and may topple. Both drought and cold resistant (hardy down to −10°C/ 14°F) it's a gardener's delight, easily propagated from cuttings or from seed after a 24 hour soaking. Flowers appear in long terminal sprays and are spicily fragrant. They pick well and make good arrangements, but do remember, like all parts of the plant, they are quite poisonous. Water with a light hand.

SPARTIUM junceum
Spanish Broom

SPIRAEA thunbergii
Thunberg Spiraea

SPIRAEA X 'Anthony Waterer'
Red May

SPIRAEA

Garland Flower,
Maybush,
May

SPRING–SUMMER
FAST/LONG DISPLAY
HT: 1-2m/3-7ft/UPRIGHT–ARCHING

☼ C T

The popular Maybushes or Garland Flowers take their principal popular name from their month of blooming in the northern hemisphere, to which they are native. A thicket of erect, often arching stems, they are not particularly eye-catching or elegant for most of the year, but come into their own in springtime, when they are almost smothered under the weight of long, arching sprays of bloom—pink, white or crimson. All species are cold hardy down to at least −5°C/23°F, and like other members of the rose family do best in a cold winter climate. They flourish in sun or part shade, acid or even slightly alkaline soil, so long as it is rich and well-drained. An occasional top-dressing of manure (say in autumn and very early spring) will help produce displays of top quality, and bloom will be prolonged by regular removal of faded flower heads. Early blooming species should be pruned immediately after flowering by thinning out and cutting away

SPIRAEA douglasii
Western Spiraea

SPIRAEA prunifolia 'Plena'
Bridal-wreath May

spindly or exhausted stems: later blooming species may be pruned at any time during winter. Stems that have flowered can be shortened right back to old wood. Most *Spiraea* species can be propagated by layering (peg down in spring, lift and cut back the following autumn). Ripe seed is another possibility, as are firm tip-cuttings taken in summer and struck in warm, humid surroundings in a mixture of damp sand and peat.

Of the illustrated species, *S. douglasii* is from western North America, produces 20cm panicles of tiny purple-rose flowers in mid-summer. *S. X* 'Anthony Waterer' is a cultivar of *S. japonica* and native to that country. The tiny, cerise blooms are borne in flat heads, often contrasting with variegated foliage. *S. thunbergii,* also from Japan and China, produces clusters of small white blooms at leaf axils and resembles Lantana; it can be pruned to a neat hedge. *S. prunifolia* 'Plena' has double white flowers the whole length of its arching branches. Both of the white-flowered species produce a worthwhile display of autumn colour in cold districts.

STACHYURUS

(no popular name)

☀ ◑
[T]

WINTER–SPRING
SLOW/LONG DISPLAY
HT: 60-300cm/2-10ft/LOOSE, SPREADING

Not cultivated long enough to have attracted any
sort of popular name, *Stachyurus* are found naturally
in Asia, but seem at home in any sort of temperate
climate. Most commonly seen *S. pracecox* is attractive at any time of year. Its branches are asymmetrical and weeping, sparsely clothed with simple,
medium-sized deciduous leaves which take on fiery
autumn tints in a cool climate. At the same time,
long chains of unopened yellow and brown blossoms
appear, looking like sections of a beaded curtain.
These gradually elongate and open, peaking just as
the spring foliage opens. Soil should be leaf-rich and
well-drained, with a generous summer water supply.
Grow from seed, or from tip-cuttings taken in late
summer and struck with mist and bottom heat.
Deadhead regularly.

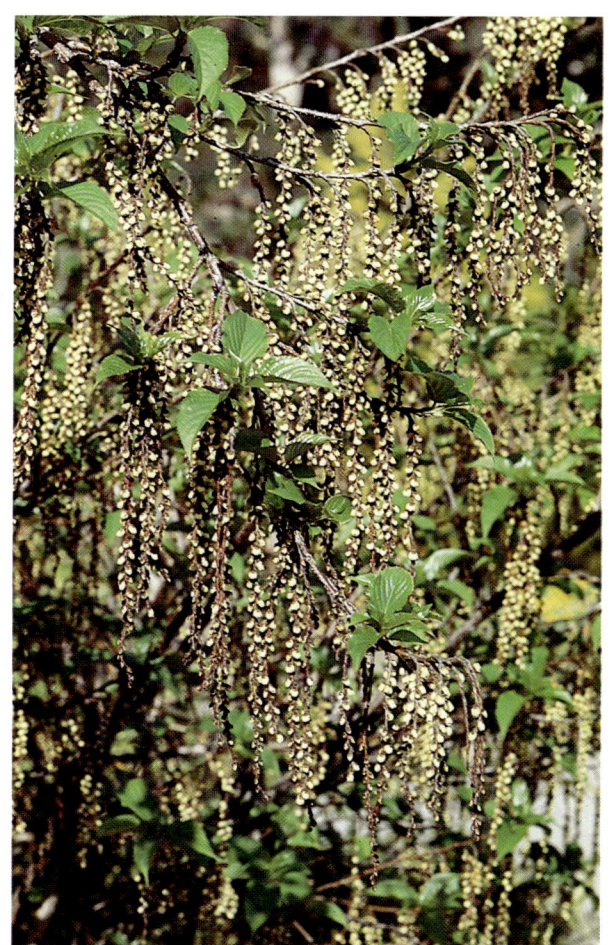

STACHYURUS praecox

STREPTOSOLEN

Marmalade Bush

☀
[T] [H]

SPRING TO ALL YEAR
FAST/LONG DISPLAY
HT: 60-200cm/2-7ft

Useful in the frost-free garden, marmalade-flowered
Streptosolen is a shrub that may turn climber or even
groundcover. The sole plant in its genus, it has
many minor variations in colour and habit. Many
weeping shoots emerge from its trunk and need
regular tip-pruning when young to help the plant
develop a shape, though it is an ideal hanging basket
subject grown as nature designed it. A light, fibrous
soil is ideal, with fast drainage and heavy summer
water both essential. Easy to grow from semi-
hardwood cuttings struck either autumn or winter
with bottom heat, *Streptosolen jamesonii* is not frost
hardy. In Australia, a very dwarf cultivar has
recently been selected. It has been named 'Ginger
Meggs'.

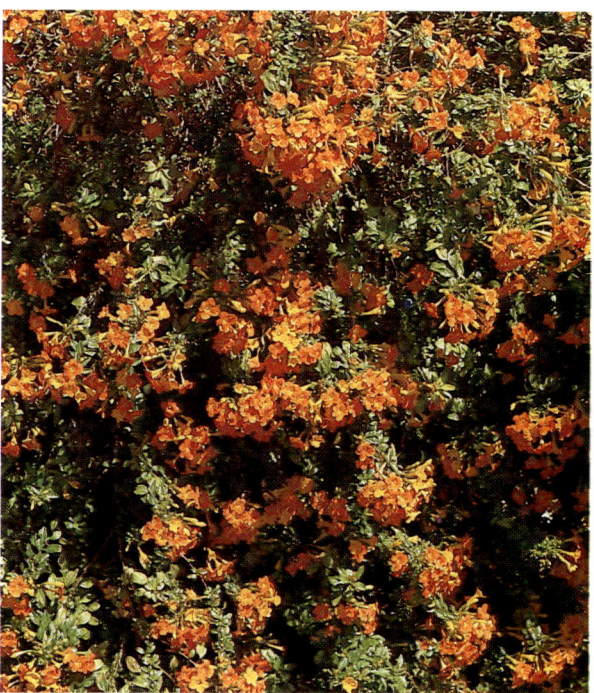

STREPTOSOLEN jamesonii
Marmalade Bush

STROPHANTHUS

Spider Tresses

SPRING–SUMMER
FAST/LONG DISPLAY
HT: 1-3.6m/3-12ft/SPRAWLING

Like so many members of the Dogbane family, (Allamanda, Mandevilla, Nerium, Plumeria) the eye-catching *Strophanthus* species are native to the tropics, and rarely seen outside warm-climate gardens. They grow best in sandy soil enriched with peat, need plenty of summer water and full sun and are definitely not frost hardy. Illustrated *S. preussii* is naturally a scrambler, but more often seen draped over a tree stump or wall. It is evergreen, with simple shining leaves that sprout from reddish stems. The 5-petalled flowers are basically cream, but shaded to orange and marked with purple streaks. The petals develop thread-like extensions up to 30cm in length. *Strophanthus* are propagated from cuttings struck under glass in moist sand. Several species are cultivated commercially for their seeds, a valuable source of cardiac drugs.

STROPHANTHUS preussii
Spider Tresses

STYPHELIA

Fivecorners

SPRING
SLOW/LONG DISPLAY
HT: 1m/3ft/SPARSE

A genus of 11 colourful species within the family Epacridaceae or Australian native heaths, the *Styphelias* will rarely be found outside their native land. Difficult of propagation, they may be raised from fresh seed with a deal of patience. Seed germination is slow and erratic, viability of cuttings not much better. All species of *Styphelia* prefer a damp, well-drained acid soil with filtered sunlight. Illustrated Pink Fivecorners (*S. triflora*) is typical, other types varying mostly in colour. The curious popular name is due to the shape created by 5 sharply reflexed petals which roll back to reveal 5 stamens protruding from a bearded interior. The shrub is woody with small, prickly leaves.

STYPHELIA triflora
Pink Fivecorners

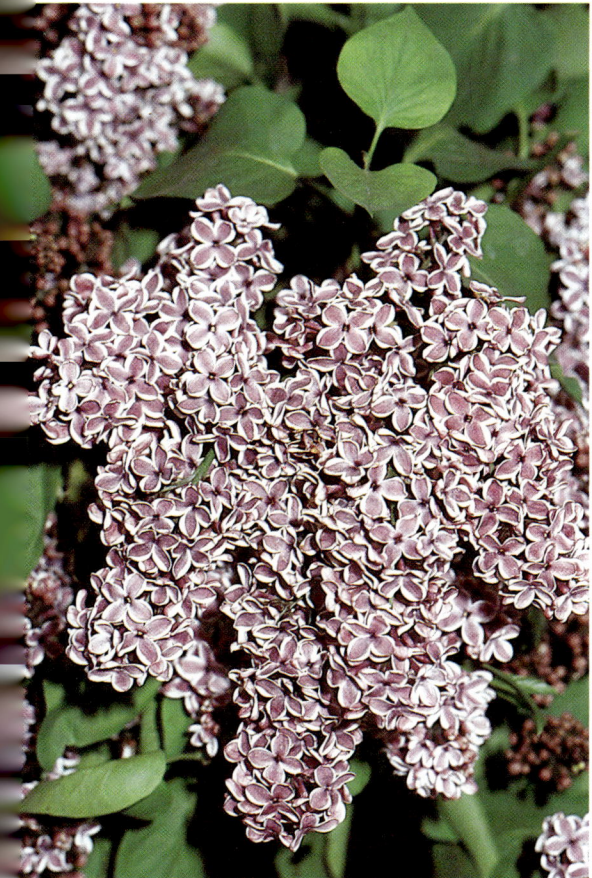

SYRINGA X 'Sensation'
Variegated Lilac

SYRINGA X *josiflexa*

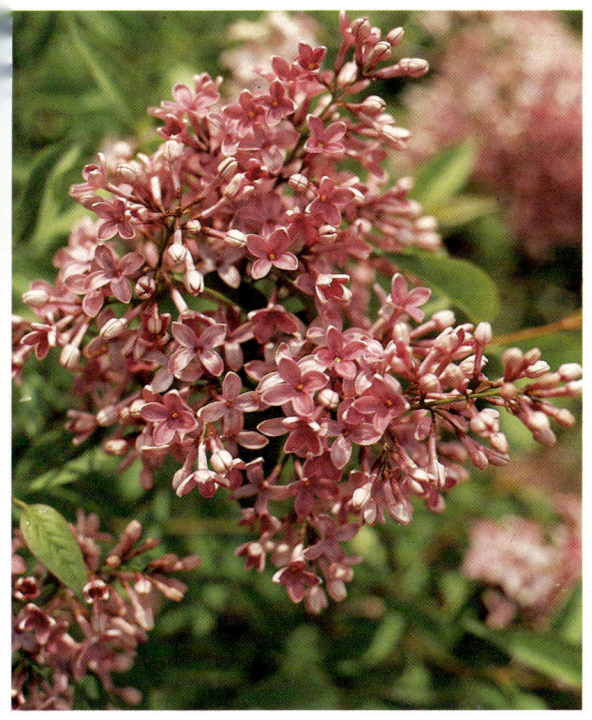

SYRINGA persica
Persian Lilac

SYRINGA

Lilac

SPRING
AVERAGE/LONG DISPLAY
HT: 2-3.6m/6-12ft/SUCKERING

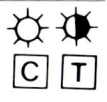

The 30-odd sweetly scented species of *Syringa* would have to be springtime's favourite shrub genus in their native northern hemisphere. Found naturally only in Europe and north-eastern Asia, they are perhaps even more popular in America's winter-frigid mid-western states, where they are among the few shrubs that can be relied on to produce a mass of springtime bloom year after year. The reason is simple. Lilacs thrive on cold. Unless they go cold-dormant they may not bloom at all the following spring. The only alternative (and not a good one at that) is to plant them in semi-shade and force them into dormancy by gradually drying them right out.

Lilacs spread from suckers and take up a lot of room. Therefore, in the smaller garden, they are

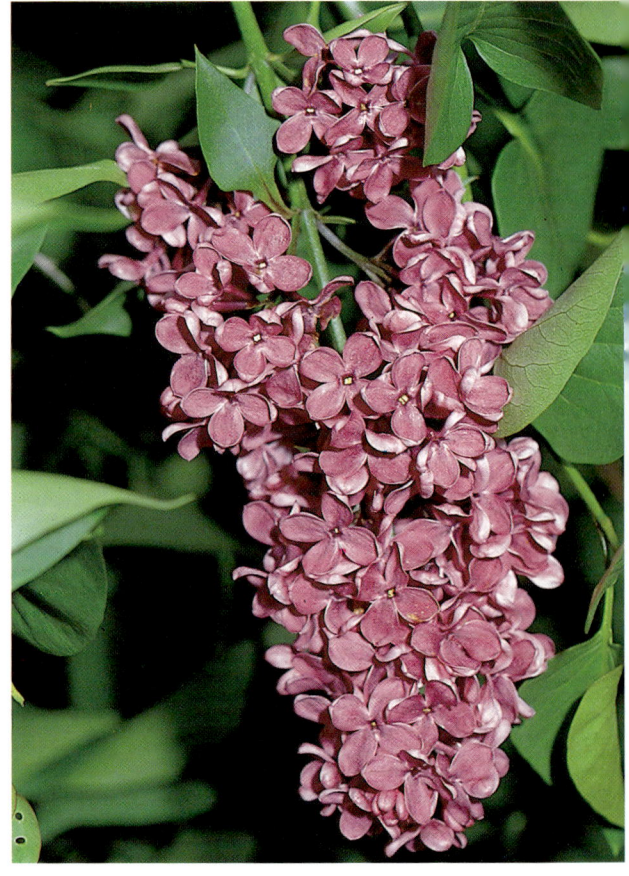

SYRINGA vulgaris
Common Lilac

SYRINGA X 'Maréchal Foch'
Lilac Cultivar

often grafted onto stock of related privet. They can be propagated from ripened seed, but will take up to 10 years with no guarantee of coming true to type. The gardener in more of a hurry will either graft onto privet stock or propagate from early summer tip-cuttings struck in a sand/peat mixture with high humidity. In mature specimens, excessive suckering should be controlled by pruning away a high proportion below soil level. Spent flower heads should be deadheaded to prevent seed formation, and a few older shoots can be pruned away altogether.

Lilacs are deciduous, mostly bearing simple, medium-sized oval leaves. An exception is *S. persica*, the Persian Lilac, which often produces 3-lobed leaves. All species produce dense panicles of 4-petalled flowers from ends of branches. These may be any shade of purple, mauve, white, pink, red-violet or primrose yellow. A leaf-rich, friable loam grows the best lilacs, but over-acid soil must be sweetened with lime. A 6-6.5 pH is ideal.

TABERNAEMONTANA FRAGRANT

Forbidden Fruit,
Eve's Apple,
Nero's Crown,
Fab Flower

SUMMER–AUTUMN
SLOW/LONG DISPLAY
HT: 1.8-3m/6-9ft/DENSE

☼ T H

The glossy leaves, faintly fragrant white periwinkle flowers and white, rubbery sap place *Tabernaemontana* in the botanical family Apocynaceae or Dogbanes. They need a semi-tropical or warmer climate, a sheltered, sunny spot, and a soil mixture of sand, loam and peat to flourish. The illustrated *T. dichotoma* or Eve's Apple is from India, has spirally twisted white, crêpy flowers and pointed, glossy, evergreen leaves. The hanging, half-round fruit has a pronounced depression along one side. This suggests a partly-eaten apple and is the origin of one of its popular names. Unlike many tropicals, water is appreciated all year.

TABERNAEMONTANA dichotoma
Forbidden Fruit

TECOMARIA

Cape Honeysuckle

SUMMER–AUTUMN
FAST/LONG DISPLAY
HT: 2-3m/6-10ft/SEMI-CLIMBING

☼ T H

Technically classed as a shrubby climber, the brassily-blooming Cape Honeysuckle, *Tecomaria capensis,* can swing either way. But if a shrub is what's wanted it must be pruned hard annually to control its long, trailing growth. Then, it is particularly useful in coastal areas, although it will tolerate drought as well as moist salt air, and can be considered hardy down to −2°C/28°F. The dark evergreen foliage is compound with 4 pairs of leaflets and an extra one at the end. The flowers, which appear in terminal sprays, are tubular and either orange or yellow, according to variety. Grow *Tecomaria* from layers or from semi-hardwood cuttings taken at any time and struck in a moist sand/peat mixture.

TECOMARIA capensis aurea
Yellow Cape Honeysuckle

TELOPEA

Waratah

SPRING
SLOW/LONG DISPLAY
HT: TO 3m/10ft/ERECT

State floral emblem of New South Wales, the gorgeous 15cm flowers of *Telopea speciosissima*, the Waratah, can be seen at a great distance in the coastal bushlands—and that is the meaning of both its botanical and Aboriginal names: 'seen from afar'. Not the easiest of plants to grow away from its own territory, it is normally raised from seed, which is sown in winter in individual pots of gritty sand and planted out when large enough. Layering may also be used for propagation when the plant is already growing. The N.S.W. Waratah prefers a damp but well-drained sandy loam with a year-round mulch of flat stones or shredded bark to ensure a cool root run. It is cold-hardy down to −8°C/17°F and can be kept compact by regular tip pruning and cutting of flowers. Leaves are spirally arranged and evergreen, toothed and leathery. The cone-like red inflorescence consists of many curved florets surrounded by a group of common bracts. Pink and greenish-white sports have been seen, but they are not yet in cultivation. Three related species are also grown. They are: *T. mongaensis*, a more open and spreading shrub with tubular scarlet flowers in loose terminal clusters about 10cm in diameter. Bloom heads should be cut to preserve a compact habit. *T. oreades*, the Gippsland Waratah, is similar to the preceding, but with larger leaves. Native to Victoria, it is popular in New Zealand gardens. Most southerly of the group is the Tasmanian Waratah *T. truncata*, again with red flowers in terminal clusters. This species has the largest leaves of all and great potential, since it has a yellow form.

TELOPEA speciosissima
Waratah

TIBOUCHINA
(syn LASIANDRA)

Glory Bush,
Princess Flower,
Quaresma

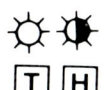

SPRING–SUMMER–AUTUMN BY SPECIES
FAST/LONG SEASON
HT: 1-5m/3-16ft/ROUNDED

Gaudy South American shrubs for acid soil that is rich and well-drained, the Lasiandras (as they are commonly called) produce extraordinary colour effects at many times of the year. New growth is shaded with bronze and red, but quickly turns to a rich, velvet green. The plants are basically evergreen, but odd leaves may turn scarlet or yellow in cold weather. The magnificent flowers most commonly appear through summer and autumn; but some species in spring. They are generally a rich, glowing purple, but pink or white species are also

TIBOUCHINA heteromalla
Glorybush

TIBOUCHINA granulosa
Princess Flower

TIBOUCHINA clavata alba
Quaresma, Silky Glory Bush

known. There are 150 or more species in the wild, but cultivars of only 3 or 4 of these are widely grown. *Tibouchina* species may be grown from fresh seed, which is raised in a mixture of sand and leaf-mould, kept continuously warm and humid. Alternatively, propagation can take place from soft tip-cuttings which can be taken any time in the warmer months and struck in a humid glasshouse. *Tibouchinas* need constant water over the warmer weather, but grow so leggy and brittle they are prone to wind damage. They should be pruned back after flowering and again in spring or late winter to promote a compact shape. Constant vigilance is needed in pinching out flyaway shoots which may grow at an extraordinary rate. Some species will take a very light frost, but would do better planted under the protection of larger trees where cold weather is to be expected regularly.

TIBOUCHINA granulosa rosea
Pink Glory Bush

TIBOUCHINA macrantha
Lasiandra

VERTICORDIA

Featherflower,
Morrison,
Juniper Myrtle

T ☼

SPRING–SUMMER
SLOW/SHORT DISPLAY
HT: 50-150cm/20-60in/ERECT

Not often seen outside their native Western
Australia, *Verticordias* are a genus of 50-odd shrubs
that should be at home anywhere the humidity is
low and the soil sandy and rich in leaf-mould. A
perfectly-drained position in full sun would seem
essential, and some success has been achieved growing them in raised beds. Still, at the present time, it
must be confessed they are shrubs for the connois-
seur, and the skilled one at that! They can be grown
from ripe seed, though fertility is low. Semi-
hardwood cuttings can be struck in a warm place
with misting. Their profusion of bloom has made
them popular in Australia's cut-flower industry, so
much so it is not surprising to find that the name
Verticordia is from the Latin 'to turn a heart'.

VERTICORDIA grandis
Scarlet Featherflower

VERTICORDIA chrysantha
Golden Featherflower

VERTICORDIA plumosa
Pink Featherflower

VIBURNUM SOME FRAGRANT

Viburnum,
Snowball

AUTUMN–SPRING
SLOW/LONG DISPLAY
HT: 30-400cm/1-13ft/VARYING

Dare one class a single genus of shrubs as the most beautiful and varied of all? It could only be said of the *Viburnums*—120 species and many more named varieties, short or tall, many with brilliant autumn foliage and colourful fruits that birds adore. Some, including *V. X burkwoodii*, *V. X carlcephalum*, *V. carlesii* and *V. tinus* have a wonderful fragrance that reminds one of honeysuckles, to whose family they belong. *Viburnums* are almost equally divided between deciduous and evergreen, but the division

VIBURNUM tinus
Laurustinus

VIBURNUM tomentosum roseum
Double-file Viburnum

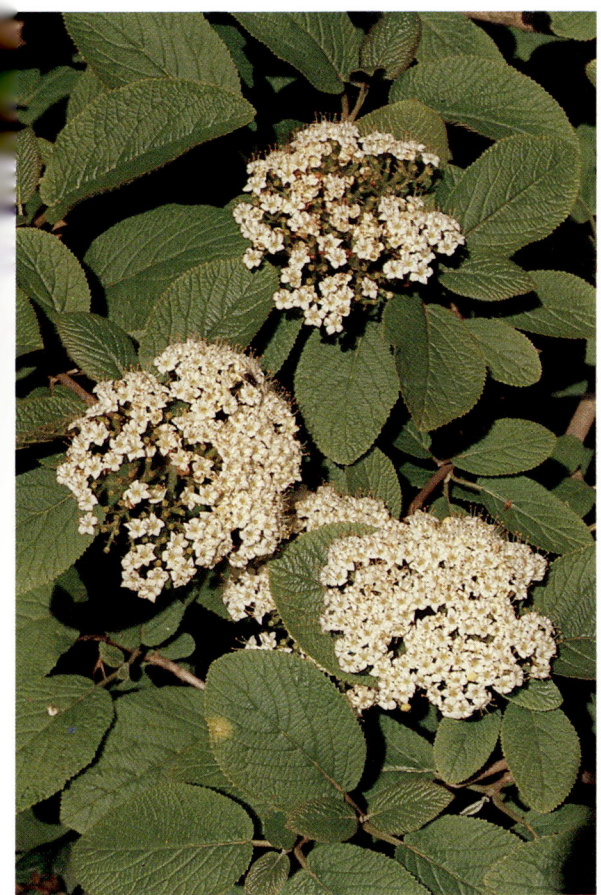

VIBURNUM X carlcephalum
Spice Flower

VIBURNUM burkwoodii
Burkwood Viburnum

can become blurred in some climates. In most species at least *some* autumn colouring can be expected, even if it is only in the fruits. All demand a moderately rich, well-drained soil and plenty of moisture throughout spring and summer. They are mostly frost-hardy and not difficult to propagate. All except a few sterile hybrids bear seed, and these often germinate naturally. Otherwise it is quite easy to strike cuttings of half-ripened shoots (most easily with gentle bottom heat) or to set layers. Many species (including illustrated *V.* X *carlcephalum* and *V. tomentosum* have rough textured leaves, others are silky on their reverses. All react adversely to sprays containing sulphur in any form, so these should be used with great care anywhere in the vicinity. Spent flower heads should be removed regularly, and an annual light pruning is wise if the plants are to be kept compact. Pests are no great problem, though mildew is often seen in seaside gardens and red spider mite elsewhere.

VIBURNUM macrocephalum
Chinese Snowball Tree

WEIGELA X 'Variegata'
Fairy Trumpets

WEIGELA X 'Bristol Ruby'
Weigelia

WEIGELA
(syn DIERVILLA)

Weigelia,
Fairy Trumpets

SPRING
FAST/SHORT DISPLAY
HT: 1.8-3m/6-10ft/UPRIGHT, ARCHING

Masses of red, white or pink trumpet flowers bring leggy *Weigelas* to life for one short season in late spring, after which they are usually cut right back to prevent their becoming untidy. The coarse, crêpy, deciduous leaves burn badly in summer sun, so *Weigelas* should be planted in part-shade or filtered light. The leaves fall early without a colour display and the shrubs are bare for a long time. If that sounds like criticism, it's quite unintentional. Though without much fragrance, the flower display is gorgeous and the arching stems cut well. Grow *Weigelas* in rich, well-drained soil and keep up the water during their period of growth, which is very fast. Propagation is best from winter cuttings of one-year-old hardwood. Strike in moist shade.

INDEX